My Country

My Country

and other poems

Dorothea Mackellar

VIKING

Viking
Penguin Books Australia Ltd
487 Maroondah Highway, PO Box 257
Ringwood, Victoria 3134, Australia
Penguin Books Ltd
Harmondsworth, Middlesex, England
Viking Penguin, A Division of Penguin Books USA Inc.
375 Hudson Street, New York, New York 10014, USA
Penguin Books Canada Limited
10 Alcorn Avenue, Toronto, Ontario, Canada M4V 3B2
Penguin Books (N.Z.) Ltd
182–190 Wairau Road, Auckland 10, New Zealand

First published by Lloyd O'Neil Pty Ltd, 1982
Reprinted 1986
First published by Penguin Books Australia Ltd, 1987
This edition published by Penguin Books Australia, 1993

10 9 8 7 6 5 4 3 2 1

Produced by Viking O'Neil,
56 Claremont Street, South Yarra, Victoria 3141, Australia,
A division of Penguin Books Australia Ltd

Designed and typeset in Australia
Printed and bound in China through Bookbuilders Ltd

National Library of Australia
Cataloguing-in-Publication data:

Mackellar, Dorothea, 1885–1968.
  My country and other poems.

  Includes index.
  ISBN 0 670 85385-2

  1. Title.

A821'.2

PUBLISHING HISTORY OF THE POEMS OF DOROTHEA MACKELLAR

The verses of Dorothea Mackellar originally were published in four separate volumes: *The Closed Door, The Witchmaid, Dreamharbour,* and *Fancy Dress.* The sections into which this book is divided bear those titles, although not all the poems have been reproduced. The aim here is to present poems which reflect the range of her work.

The Closed Door was published by the Australasian Authors' Agency, Melbourne, in 1911, and contained verses which originally had appeared in the London *Spectator*; the Sydney *Bulletin; Harper's Magazine; Sunday Times; Bush Brother; Southern Sphere;* and *Appleton's Magazine.*

The Witchmaid was first published by J. M. Dent & Sons Ltd, London, in 1914. Some of its verses had appeared in *The Closed Door;* others had been published in the *Spectator* and the Sydney *Bulletin.*

Dreamharbour was first published by Longmans, Green and Co., London, in 1923. A number of its verses originally appeared in *Harpers Magazine; Poetry; Birth;* the *Forum; Art in Australia;* the Sydney *Bulletin;* the *Triad;* and the *Australasian* and *Sunday Mail.*

Fancy Dress was first published by Angus & Robertson Ltd, Sydney, in 1926. It contained verses which had appeared in the *Sydney Morning Herald;* the *Bulletin; Forum; Melbourne Punch; Spinner; Woman's Mirror;* and other periodicals which have not been traced.

CONTENTS

2

DOROTHEA MACKELLAR
A MEMOIR BY ADRIENNE MATZENIK

When I first met Dorothea Mackellar, I was deeply impressed by her musical voice, her regal carriage and the bright, alert, somewhat prominent hazel eyes, which seemed to see more deeply than those of other people.

I listened in fascination to the many stories which she told me, of a life which began in the colonial days of Australia. Though warm-hearted, generous, and kind, she could be sharp tongued when the occasion required. She told me of how, when she attended one of her first balls, she overheard a friend offering to introduce her to a stranger. The stranger said: 'Righto. Let's get it over. Trot her out,' so when the introduction had been made she turned to her friend and said, 'Righto. You can trot him off now.'

She was born on 1 July 1885, at her family's home on Point Piper, Sydney. The third of four children born to Doctor Charles Mackellar and his wife Marion, and the only girl, she was christened Isobel Marion Dorothea Mackellar.

She was a member of a well-known and wealthy family. Her father, the son of a doctor and landowner, was born at Sydney in 1844, studied medicine at Glasgow University, and returned to Australia to establish a very successful practice. He became a member of the Legislative Council of New South Wales, on which he sat for forty years, and in 1903 was appointed a Federal senator. His special interests were in public health and the then almost untouched fields of juvenile delinquency and mentally defective children, on which he wrote articles and pamphlets. His work was recognised with a knighthood in 1912 and appointment as K.C.M.G. in 1916, and he died in 1926.

Her mother was a daughter of Sir Thomas Buckland, the Sydney financier and philanthropist whose lifespan stretched from 1848 to 1947. His activities included goldmining, banking, insurance, and real estate, and his many munificent gifts to the public included the purchase of a bomber for the R.A.A.F. in 1940.

With such a background, Dorothea Mackellar was brought up in all the spacious and protected comfort of a wealthy family in the Victorian era. Most of her early life was spent in the family home, Dunara, which stood on the eastern side of Point Piper overlooking Rose Bay. The large house was surrounded by a huge garden of which part had been cultivated, part left as virgin bush, so that her earliest memories were of bushland and seashore — the themes which recur so often in her work.

Her family also owned country properties at various times, and she and her brothers spent long holidays on these. She became an ardent horsewoman and animal lover, and for much of her life owned several dogs.

Very early in life, she showed signs of great intellectual facility. She taught herself to read at the age of four, and from then onwards she was privately educated until she began to attend University lectures. She went to a kind of private kindergarten with the children of the Governor, and then was taught by a governess. Later she had special tutors in painting, languages, and fencing — the latter an Italian who had fought under Garibaldi.

She revealed a natural gift for languages which was noticed by Sir William McGregor, a close friend of Doctor Mackellar, who urged him to encourage this talent. Consequently she became fluent in French, German, Spanish, and Italian, and acted as translator for her father during his work and travels.

Apart from education by others, she was continually and almost unconsciously educating herself. She was an alert and inquisitive child, who resented the time that had to be spent in sleep, and whenever she was put to bed she would try to stay awake by repeating every rhyme or adage she had read or been taught. This developed a gift which she retained until the last months of her life: an amazing memory for dialogue and verse.

In about 1900, Doctor Mackellar bought Torryburn: a property on the Allyn River near Patterson, New South Wales.

This is a serenely beautiful district which in those days abounded with wild life: wombats, possums, platypuses, and countless birds and insects. Dorothea revelled in the country life, even during the droughts which dried up the creeks and caused the bare soil to crack like crazy paving.

When one of these droughts was at last broken, Dorothea saw how a mist of green began to appear upon the parched land, seeming to thicken as she watched. Her joy in the rain caused her to kick off her shoes and run out to dance in it. The incident was still fresh in her mind when, at nineteen, she wrote the best-known and best-loved of her works: *My Country*.

Such awakening joy in life was shadowed by the sadness of losing her brother Keith, who volunteered for service in the South African War and died when only nineteen. Her father endowed the Keith Mackellar Ward, in Sydney's Prince Alfred Hospital, in his memory. Even at the end of her life Dorothea could not speak of him without emotion.

Dorothea Mackellar began to write for publication in her adolescence. There were many more 'markets' for young writers in those days. Reading was one of the main relaxations, and was catered for by a host of newspapers and magazines — most of which have long since disappeared. She was successful in selling the paragraphs, short verses, and anecdotes which magazines used as 'fillers' and then received the accolade of acceptance by the American magazine *Harper's*, which published her poem *An Old Song*. Her family received the news with mixed feelings. Her brother Eric was stunned by the amount she was paid, while her mother was most concerned lest the concluding lines, 'I never had but one love/ And he died, yesterday,' meant that her daughter was nursing a broken heart.

The poem was only that of a romantic girl, but soon afterwards she did fall in love. It was with an older married man, a friend of her father's, so she was often in his company. It had to be one of those silent affairs which nevertheless are intense with the yearnings of a healthy young body and a warm, questing heart, but found expression in some of her most intense romantic lyric verse.

Her work began to appear in well-regarded journals such as the London *Spectator* and the Sydney *Bulletin,* and it was at about this time that she became engaged to be married. She would not have been looked upon as a pretty girl in those days when chocolate box beauties were most admired, but she had the handsome features which were still apparent so many years later, allied to great physical fitness and the sparkle of ardent intelligence which always enlivened her expression.

The engagement did not last long. She had been invited to Brisbane, to attend an official function at which naval officers from the American 'Great White Fleet,' which was at that time touring the world, would be present. Her fiance objected to her attending without him, and without argument she gave him back the ring. 'If he had so little trust in me that he thought I would fall into the arms of the first sailor who made advances, I did not want to know him, much less marry him,' she told me.

Her first collection of verse, *The Closed Door,* was published in 1911. In 1912, her first novel appeared: *The Little Blue Devil,* written in collaboration with Ruth Bedford. In 1913, Mills & Boon published her *Outlaw's Luck,* and in 1914 she wrote another book with Ruth Bedford: *Two's Company.* The three books were light novels of adventure, and made no great impact.

Most of her work was written during the first three decades of this century, and was inspired by her own country, by her travels overseas — which began at the age of two, because Doctor Mackellar believed that travel was part of education, and took his family with him on his journeys — and by all 'emotion recollected in tranquillity' which Tennyson said was the driving force of the poet.

Her imagination was a blend of the practical and romantic. She put much of her early experience into verse, finding emotional outlet in the rhythm of words and phrases. Her deep

7

love for Australia made her resent an attitude which was common in her youth: the tendency of her acquaintances to disparage Australia and to refer to England as 'Home'. She knew that those who affected to despise the 'wide brown land' owed their wealth and comfort to its people and resources, and disliked the way in which they compared it adversely with England. Such feelings made the evocative lines of *My Country* begin to take shape in her mind.

She knew England well, and loved many of its aspects. Apart from visits with her father, she lived there for some years before World War I in company with her friend and collaborator Ruth Bedford. She met and became very friendly with Joseph Conrad and his wife, and while living in London she and Ruth wrote a letter of appreciation to Patrick Chalmers, a poet whose work they had enjoyed. They met, and Patrick and Dorothea soon fell in love. He was a banker, wealthy, discriminating, and sensitive; she was a woman of twenty-eight, overflowing with romantic passion. They became engaged, and she asked only that he allow her to return to Australia to tell her parents of the arrangements.

She had just arrived home when World War I broke out. She wrote to Chalmers to tell him of her parents' approval, then plunged into war work while she waited for his reply. The months passed, and she tried to tell herself that his letter had been delayed by war conditions. It is difficult, nowadays, to imagine the upbringing which laid such stress upon female modesty that she was virtually incapable of making any further advances. But when she did not hear from him, she did not write again, and decided that his love had not stood the test of parting.

She endured the inner anguish of her heart amidst the greater anguish of a world at war, but when peace had come she could not resist making another voyage to England. Five years had passed; she did not even know whether he was still alive. But he was. He had not received her letter; he had assumed that she had changed her mind and had married another woman.

She was forced to behave as though they had never been more than acquaintances. He told her that he found her much changed: colder and harder. 'Do you think I am less than human?' she asked.

Later, she found and translated the Spanish *dolora* which, from what she said to me, expressed her feelings for Patrick to the end. It concludes: 'I forgive with all my heart/Even those I hated lately: You, whom I have loved so greatly/Never will I pardon you!'

It was in this period that some of her verse took on a deeper and more tragic tone. *Sorrow*, which with its lacerating lines tears at the heart, is a far cry from the idyllic romanticism of her verse written in girlhood. She was thirty-three, but she was at least more fortunate than some other women who had found themselves in the same position. There was the beauty of the world for consolation, and the ability to translate her emotions to another kind of beauty.

By that time, her best-known poem *My Country* had been known and loved for fourteen years. She had begun it during an earlier visit to England, when her nostalgia for Australia was made sharper by hearing her friends praising the soft beauty of the English countryside. She was not happy with the verses, and worked over them several times until she completed a final draft while living in Buckland Chambers, Sydney: an apartment which her family occupied because they had let Dunara while touring overseas. The building was old and shabby when I saw it last, and for all I know may have been pulled down by this time. It was poignant to imagine the young Dorothea Mackellar, in all the vigour of her youth, sitting in her room upstairs and poring over *My Country*; always dissatisfied with it because she did not feel that it gave the deepest and truest expression to her love for her country.

Because of this dissatisfaction she hesitated to submit it for publication, but when she did so it was acclaimed at once. It has been reprinted, recited, set to music, and sung innumerable times. In 1918, it was reproduced with special illustrations and decorations in the book *The Art of J. J. Hilder*. From time to

9

time, there have been suggestions that it should be adopted as Australia's national anthem.

And yet, more than fifty years after she wrote it, she told me, 'I never professed to be a poet. I have written — from the heart, from imagination, from experience — some amount of verse. All I can say of *My Country* is that I wrote it with sincerity.'

During the 1920s and early 1930s she continued to write and to travel, but suffered increasing ill-health. With her parents dead and her brothers in homes of their own, she acquired two houses: one at Lovett Bay, on the Pittwater, and a town house called Cintra, built in the 1830s on the Darling Point Road. While she was in hospital, real estate agents wrote assuming that she would be willing to accept a 'most generous offer' for Cintra: an approach which she rejected with scorn.

Eventually she spent over ten years in Helenie Hospital, Randwick, but this was not a period of oblivion. On her birthdays, her room was massed with flowers and cards from admirers, and such tokens arrived steadily throughout the years.

Her love of nature betrayed her in the end. She had gone back to live at Cintra, and disobeyed doctor's orders by getting out of bed to 'watch the birds and insects' in the trees outside her window. She fell, and had to be taken to the Scottish Hospital at Paddington, where she died on 14 February 1968. She had outlived all her family, and since her two brothers died without leaving heirs, there is no one left to carry on the name of that branch of the Mackellar line.

It has been said that 'the life of a poet can never be happy, because he feels too deeply.' One can never know the true feelings of another, but from her many long talks with me I believe that Dorothea Mackellar knew great joys as well as deep sorrow in her life. Many of her poems reflect the delight which she took in the beauty of the world; many of her conversations revealed the pleasure with which she looked back upon her early life. 'If I am tired I call on these to help me to dream,' she said in her poem *Colour*, and I think that until the end of her days she could know happiness more intense than is given to most people to enjoy.

THE CLOSED DOOR

MY COUNTRY

The love of field and coppice,
  Of green and shaded lanes,
Of ordered woods and gardens
  Is running in your veins.
Strong love of grey-blue distance,
  Brown streams and soft, dim skies —
I know but cannot share it,
  My love is otherwise.

I love a sunburnt country,
  A land of sweeping plains,
Of ragged mountain ranges,
  Of droughts and flooding rains.
I love her far horizons,
  I love her jewel-sea,
Her beauty and her terror —
  The wide brown land for me!

The stark white ring-barked forests,
  All tragic to the moon,
The sapphire-misted mountains,
  The hot gold hush of noon.
Green tangle of the brushes,
  Where lithe lianas coil,
And orchids deck the tree tops
  And ferns the warm dark soil.

11

Core of my heart, my country!
  Her pitiless blue sky,
When sick at heart, around us,
  We see the cattle die —
But then the grey clouds gather,
  And we can bless again
The drumming of an army,
  The steady, soaking rain.

Core of my heart, my country!
  Land of the Rainbow Gold,
For flood and fire and famine,
  She pays us back three-fold.
Over the thirsty paddocks,
  Watch, after many days,
The filmy veil of greenness
  That thickens as we gaze . . .

An opal-hearted country,
  A wilful, lavish land —
All you who have not loved her,
  You will not understand —
Though earth holds many splendours,
  Wherever I may die,
I know to what brown country
  My homing thoughts will fly.

THE OPEN SEA

From my window I can see,
Where the sandhills dip,
One far glimpse of open sea.
Just a slender slip
Curving like a crescent moon —
Yet a greater prize

12

Than the harbour garden-fair
Spread beneath my eyes.

Just below me swings the bay,
Sings a sunny tune,
But my heart is far away
Out beyond the dune;
Clearer far the sea-gulls' cry
And the breakers' roar,
Than the little waves beneath
Lapping on the shore.

For that strip of sapphire sea
Set against the sky,
Far horizons means to me —
And the ships go by
Framed between the empty sky
And the yellow sands,
While my freed thoughts follow them
Out to the other lands.

All its changes who can tell?
I have seen it shine
Like a jewel polished well,
Hard and clear and fine;
Then soft lilac — and again
On another day
Glimpsed it through a veil of rain,
Shifting, drifting grey.

When the livid waters flee,
Flinching from the storm,
From my window I can see,
Standing safe and warm,
How the white foam tosses high
On the naked shore,

And the breakers' thunder grows
To a battle-roar. . . .

Far and far I look — Ten miles?
No, for yesterday
Sure I saw the Blessed Isles
Twenty worlds away.
My blue moon of open sea,
Is it little worth?
At the least it gives to me
Keys of all the earth!

THE GREY LAKE

Far away to southward
    The grey lake lies,
Thirty leagues of mud, bare
    To turquoise skies.

Shallow, sluggish water
    Warm — warm as blood,
Not enough to cover
    The quaking mud.

Hot winds drive the water
    In summer time,
Southward — and behind them
    There lies grey slime.

Forty miles to westward,
    A hundred north,
Wind-fiends hunt the water
    Back — back and forth.

There are reed-grown islands,
  The eye scarce sees,
Grey ooze guarding grimly
  Their mysteries.

Strange Things may survive there,
  What, who can tell?
Monsters old — the lake-slime
  Can guard them well.

No one knows those islands,
  The gulls that fly,
May go near, but others
  Would surely die.

For the wind-scourged water
  Would flee the ships,
And the mud would open
  Her soft smooth lips. . . .

So the isles are sacred
  From alien tread,
Since the slime can swallow
  And keep her dead.

Who can know her secrets?
  The blue sky might —
(Cloudless-hot in daytime
  Star-gemmed at night).

To and fro for ever
  The water swings,
And the gulls fly over,
  For *they* have wings.

COLOUR

The lovely things that I have watched unthinking,
    Unknowing, day by day,
That their soft dyes had steeped my soul in colour
    That will not pass away:—

Great saffron sunset clouds, and larkspur mountains,
    And fenceless miles of plain,
And hillsides golden-green in that unearthly
    Clear shining after rain;

And nights of blue and pearl, and long smooth beaches,
    Yellow as sunburnt wheat,
Edged with a line of foam that creams and hisses,
    Enticing weary feet.

And emeralds, and sunset-hearted opals,
    And Asian marble, veined
With scarlet flame, and cool green jade, and moonstones
    Misty and azure-stained;

And almond trees in bloom, and oleanders,
    Or a wide purple sea,
Of plain-land gorgeous with a lovely poison,
    The evil Darling pea.

If I am tired I call on these to help me
    To dream — and dawn-lit skies,
Lemon and pink, or faintest, coolest lilac,
    Float on my soothed eyes.

There is no night so black but you shine through it,
    There is no morn so drear,
O Colour of the World, but I can find you,
    Most tender, pure and clear.

Thanks be to God, Who gave this gift of colour,
  Which who shall seek shall find;
Thanks be to God, Who gives me strength to hold it,
  Though I were stricken blind.

SETTLERS

If the gods of Hellas do not tread our shaggy mountains —
Stately, white-and-golden, with unfathomable eyes:—
Yet the lesser spirits haunt our forests and our fountains,
Seas and green-brown river-pools no thirsty summer dries.

Never through the tangled scrub we see Diana glisten,
Silver-limbed and crescent-crowned and swift to hear and turn,
When the chase is hottest and the woods are waked to listen,
While her maidens follow running knee-deep in the fern.

Of the great gods only Pan walks hourly here — Pan only,
In the warm, dark gullies, in the thin clear upland air,
On the windy sea-cliffs and the plains apart and lonely,
By the tingling silence you may know that he is there.

But the sea nymphs make our shores shine gay with light and laughter,
At the sunset when the waves are mingled milk and fire,
You may see them very plain, and in the darkness after,
You may hear them singing with the stars' great golden choir.

When the earth is mad with song some blue September morning,
In the grove of myall trees that rustle green and grey,
Through the plumes of trailing leaves hung meet for her adorning,
See a dark-browned Dryad peep, and swiftly draw away!

In the deep-cut river beds set thick with moss-grown boulders,
Where the wagtails come to drink and balance lest they fall,

You may see the gleaming of a Naiad's slippery shoulders,
And the water sliding cool and quiet over all.

Through the narrow gorges where the flying foxes muster,
Hanging from the kurrajongs like monstrous magic grapes,
Something spreads a sudden fear that breaks each heavy cluster —
See the furry prick-eared faun that chuckles and escapes!

Marble-smooth and marble-pale the blue gums guard the clearing,
Where the winter fern is gold among the silver grass,
And the shy bush creatures watching bright-eyed and unfearing,
See the slender Oreads while we unheeding pass.

Wreathed with starry clematis these tread the grassy spaces,
When the moon sails up beyond the highest screening tree,
All the forest dances, and the furthest hidden places
Are astir with beauty — but we may not often see.

Centuries before the golden vision came to find us,
Showing us the Southern lands, these Grecians settled here:
Now they throng the country, but our little hurries blind us,
And we must be reverent ere the least of them appear.

RUNNING WATER

Under the bridge the water
Ripples and smooths and swirls,
Plaits and eddies and dimples,
Chuckles and lisps and purls,
Lapping the polished arches,
Hurrying out of sight,
Swift, with a sound like kisses,
Into the growing night.

Here by the bridge the sunshine,
Throwing the last soft gleam,
Flings down a net of jewels
Over the little stream.
Laughing the water meets it,
Loves it, but will not stay,
Into the rising shadows,
Hastening far away.

Under the bridge it gurgles,
Greener than emeralds are,
Innocent crystal water —
But, ere it travels far,
There where the shadows veil it,
Is not the portent strange?
Evil its voice and aspect,
Witched to a wicked change.

.   .   .   .   .   .

Night has risen around us,
Even the shining sky,
Darkens at last, the water,
Almost unseen flows by.
Quieter now its voice is,
Sinister, subtle, cold,
Whispering from the dimness,
Things that may not be told.

Some sweet devil is in it,
Soul of a lithe young witch,
Now that it hurries onward,
Black as a stream of pitch,
Black as her long hair flowing —
Save that a drowning spark
Shows where a star reflected
Glitters amid the dark.

Under the bridge the water
Whispers and laughs and sings,
Soft on the wet stone arches,
Telling of secret things.
Young and pure in the sunshine,
Ageless and black at night,
Ever the water hurries,
Rapt in an endless flight.

CULGAI PADDOCK

I know that the tawny grass of the plain
　　Is blown like the sea today,
By the wind that follows the autumn rain
　　And chases the clouds away.

And ruffles the winding lagoon, and now
　　The sky's blue, dewy and clean,
Will show in the lee where the rushes bow
　　Like shattered aquamarine.

Today, when the cranes in their grey and pink
　　Fish solemnly in the weeds,
Today, when the cattle come down to drink
　　And push through the whispering reeds.

I stand there and watch them, in Culgai, too,
　　And they do not heed or fear.
There is not one lark in the radiant blue
　　Whose carol I do not hear.

This morning the wind on the grasses brown
　　Blows tingling and sweet and rare.
Now, though my body must tarry in town,
　　Thank God that my soul is there!

SKETCH

From the little balcony
High above the street, I see,
After sunset, how the park
Changes in the growing dark.
For by day the flowers show,
Scarlet salvia row on row,
Oleander, tamarisk,
Flaming near the Obelisk;
Frank blue sky and fair green grass,
Smile a welcome as we pass.

But at set of sun behold
Shining bubbles all of gold,
Hanging from the altered trees —
What strange magic gave us these?
Are they golden fruit of night,
Shedding an enchanted light?
For the grass shows greener far
Here than earthly grasses are.
From some stage-land forest scene
Comes that wild and hectic green.

Down the centre of the park,
Like toy trees from Noah's ark,
Stand the fig-trees lopped last spring,
And the fresh leaves bourgeoning,
Straight from out the trunks, show bright
Polished in the stagey light.
Everywhere that light has made
Pools of colour, shores of shade,
Till familiar corners seem
Vague, remote as in a dream.

From the balcony by day
One sees very far away,

21

But when sunset colours die
One by one upon the sky,
Then the boundaries extend
Till the witch-park has no end.
It could reach to touch a star
Never daylight showed so far.
Yet at dawn it wakens plain,
Unbewitched and frank again.

Those gold apples of the dark,
Change the spirit of the park.

BLUE AND SILVER

Here I lie on the windy hill,
   Leaning back on a tilted stone,
Gazing over the wide clear plain,
   Very happy and all alone.

Silver grass on the shining plain,
   Silver clouds in the brilliant sky,
All around me the thin cool air —
   Surely a bird must feel as I!

I am poised in the crystal air,
   Looking down to the plain below;
Brown-red dots in the silver grass,
   Very slowly the cattle go.

Silver clouds, great as half the sky —
   I could touch them, I am so near,
Held in the wind's own cool embrace:—
   Undisputed I throne it here.

Silver clouds on the stainless blue,
    Silver plain where the cattle feed —
From the hill in the wind and sun,
    Both seem equally far, indeed.

This is only a little hill,
    I have climbed it, and well I know;
Yet I listen and close my eyes —
    Hark, the round earth spinning below!

Silver grass on the level plain,
    Silver clouds in the dazzling sky —
I have left my body behind,
    If I tried I could surely fly!

THE COORONG SANDHILLS

Over the Coorong sandhills only the wild duck fly,
    Naught is there but the knot-grass rank, and the sea, and the sky.
Redder than cooling lava, slow heave the hills to the blue,
    Splendid, dazzling, and stainless, of sky and of ocean, too.

South to the frozen mountains faces the last red hill,
    Only the sea between them: almost as lone and still,
Shows the sand as the ice-peaks, but it has heat and light,
    Set against the aurora that shatters the polar night.

If the sands have a language, healing it is and kind,
    Clean and strong like the sea-roar, or the glad shout of the wind.
If you but face them bravely, lost in a barren land,
    Never will they betray you, the sky and the sea and sand.

Blue burns the sky above me, red the sand at my feet,
    Near and far on the sandhills shimmers the living heat:

Hill after hill I conquer, changing yet still the same,
   Still flows the sand together and covers the way I came.

Stretched in a warm sand-hollow, late in the afternoon,
   Watch I the wild duck flying back to the long lagoon.
Black on an amber sunset passes the last of the flight —
   Over the Coorong sandhills quiver the pinions of night.

FIRE

This life that we call our own
Is neither strong nor free:
A flame in the wind of death,
It trembles ceaselessly.

And this all we can do
To use our little light
Before, in the piercing wind,
It flickers into night:

To yield the heat of the flame,
To grudge not, but to give
Whatever we have of strength,
That one more flame may live.

BURNING OFF

They're burning off at the Rampadells,
   The tawny flames uprise,
With greedy licking around the trees:
   The fierce breath sears our eyes.

From cores already grown furnace-hot —
   The logs are well alight!

We fling more wood where the flameless heart
    Is throbbing red and white.

The fire bites deep in that beating heart,
    The creamy smoke-wreaths ooze
From cracks and knot-holes along the trunk
    To melt in greys and blues.

.   .   .   .   .

The young horned moon has gone from the sky,
    And night has settled down;
A red glare shows from the Rampadells,
    Grim as a burning town:

Full seven fathoms above the rest
    A tree stands, great and old,
A red-hot column whence fly the sparks,
    One ceaseless shower of gold.

All hail the king of the fire before
    He sway and crack and crash
To earth — for surely tomorrow's sun
    Will see him white fine ash.

The king in his robe of falling stars,
    No trace shall leave behind,
And where he stood with his silent court,
    The wheat shall bow to the wind.

MAGIC

Crawling up the hillside,
    Swinging round the bay,
With a ceaseless humming,
    Ply the trams all day.

When it's dark I linger
  Just to see the sight;
All those jewelled beetles
  Flashing through the night!

Anything more lovely
  I have never seen
Than the sparks above them,
  White and blue and green;

Sometimes they are tiny:
  In a storm they shine,
Dragons' tongues that follow
  All along the line!

When the wind has fallen,
  And the bay's like glass,
Would you see some magic?
  Watch what comes to pass:

There is just a ripple
  Where the water breaks,
All the lamps reflected
  Show like golden snakes:

Wait, the tram is coming
  Round the curving shore,
And its humming changes
  To a hollow roar:

There's a flaming glory
  On the bay at last,
Red and green and orange —
  It has come, and passed.

Nothing breaks the stillness,
  All is as before,

And the golden serpents
Quiver near the shore. . . .

Trams are only ugly
Passing day by day,
But at night their crudeness
Vanishes away.

Some kind magic clothes them
In a fairer dress,
So that we may wonder
At their loveliness!

IN A SOUTHERN GARDEN

When the tall bamboos are clicking to the restless little breeze,
And bats begin their jerky skimming flight,
And the creamy scented blossoms of the dark pittosporum trees,
Grow sweeter with the coming of the night.

And the harbour in the distance lies beneath a purple pall,
And nearer, at the garden's lowest fringe,
Loud the water soughs and gurgles 'mid the rocks below the wall,
Dark-heaving, with a dim uncanny tinge

Of a green as pale as beryls, like the strange faint-coloured flame
That burns around the Women of the Sea:
And the strip of sky to westward which the camphor-laurels frame,
Has turned to ash-of rose and ivory —

And a chorus rises valiantly from where the crickets hide,
Close-shaded by the balsams drooping down —
It is evening in a garden by the kindly waterside,
A garden near the lights of Sydney town!

SPRING ON THE PLAINS

Spring has come to the plains,
And, following close behind,
Green of the welcome rains
And spice of the first warm wind.
Beating of wings on high,
For, overhead in the blue,
Southward the brolgas fly,
The cranes and pelicans, too,
Ibis and proud black swan —
And quivering cries float clear,
After the birds are gone,
Still lingering in the ear.

Everywhere we pass
The horses tread soft and deep;
Clover and young green grass —
Hark to the grazing sheep
Cropping steady and slow —
A peaceful, satisfied sound:
Thick on the paths we go,
Gold flowers are starring the ground.
Spring, and the world's astir,
And everything gives praise,
Singing the strength of her
These lovely lengthening days.

NIGHT ON THE PLAINS

Out here on the plain-land at night
  There is no sound, not a sigh;
And nothing is moving now
  But scornful stars in the sky:

The night is too great for my heart,
  It flutters and halts and trips,
The terrible mirth of the stars
  Has slain my song on my lips.

THE GATES OF EL DORADO

Jade-green trees and golden grass,
Autumn roses passionate,
From them all I needs must pass,
Let me linger at the gate!
        Let me wait a little yet,
        So that I shall not forget.

Glory when the sun goes down,
Stars a steady blaze of white,
Till the moon swims up to drown
Hill and plain in silver light —
        Let me look and look, until
        Sure my heart will hold it still.

So I halt before I go
At the gate, and see again
That Dream-Country flush and glow,
El Dorado, growing plain:
        El Dorado, always fair,
        As it was when I was there.

29

THE NIGHT WIND

The wind is going about the house,
   Round and round and round,
Out in the dark of a starless night,
   With a very lonely sound:

And telling of all the things that were,
   All the things to be.
It bears no hope or comfort or rest —
   But it doesn't frighten me!

For while I have these who love me so,
   These I love so well,
Love that will last — is there aught to fear
   In Earth or Heaven or Hell?
(*Touch wood!*)
   In Earth or Heaven or Hell?

THE DREAMER

Over the crest of the Hill of Sleep,
Over the plain where the mists lie deep,
Into a country of wondrous things,
Enter we dreaming, and know we're kings.

Murmur or roar as it may, the stream
Laughs to the youngster who dreams his dream.
Leave him alone till his fool's heart breaks:
Dreams all are real till the dreamer wakes!

DAWN

At the dawning of the day,
On the road into Gunnedah,
When the sky is pink and grey
As the wings of a wild galah,
And the last night-shadow ebbs
From the trees like a falling tide,
And the dew-hung spiderwebs
On the grass-blades spread far and wide —
Each sharp spike loaded well,
Bent down low with the heavy dew —
Wait the daily miracle
When the world is all made anew:
When the sun's rim lifts beyond
The horizon turned crystal-white,
And a sea of diamond
Is the plain to the dazzled sight. . . .

At the dawning of the day,
To my happiness thus it fell:
That I went the common way,
And I witnessed a miracle.

LOST DAYS

The days I lost in dreaming, when my head was turned away,
When I saw not the sunlight or the ripples on the Bay,
The days I chose to forfeit when I held myself in gaol —
The sweet lost days I wasted then, I live them now full tale!

They are not wholly wasted though, those days of needless pain,
For I have learnt my lesson, I shall not err again,
I could not err in *that* way, now, whatever else I do,
For I am young and strong and sane, and people love me, too!

31

I lie upon my back and watch the small white clouds race by,
High up and hard and shining on the soft blue of the sky —
I have the seen world at my will, clear-eyed and young and strong,
The tide of life runs in my veins, naught can be wholly wrong!

Midsummer days, midsummer days — what is't the old song sings?
Midsummer nights, midsummer nights, I dream of wondrous things. . . .
Lost hours that once I forfeited, with all their chance of bliss,
Grey nightmare time! it's worth it all, if waking is like this!

UP COUNTRY

Beyond the yellow levels,
The belt of dark belar
That edges the horizon
There is a land afar.
A land of hope and promise,
A land of sweat and toil,
A land of hidden waters,
And warm rich crumbling soil.

The burden of the summer,
That leaves the cracked earth bare,
Yet has no power to stifle
The life that slumbers there.
And when the sky's hard splendour
Has changed to grey again,
The cool soft grey of rain-clouds
Low-hanging to the plain.

And walls of rain close round us —
Then surely at our feet
The hidden life is stirring
To waken green and sweet.
And if we have no autumn,

As people sometimes say,
And only very seldom
We know a winter's day —

(O, bitter wind of winter
That pierces to the bone!
We have no snow, but surely
A winter of our own) —
See, how the sap is thrilling
In every growing thing!
They know not what they speak of
Who say we have no spring.

Beyond the distant skyline,
(Now pansy-blue and clear),
We know a land is waiting,
A brown land, very dear.
A land of open spaces,
Gaunt forest, treeless plain:
And if we once have loved it
We must come back again.

THE WITCHMAID

HIGH PLACES

My heart turns to the mountains
That I so long have missed,
The blue hills on the sky-line,
Bird-haunted, sunshine-kissed;
For in my soul I see them,
The gullies golden-green
Where from the hop-vine tangle
The bellbird chimes unseen.

And higher yet and higher
I want to climb, until
The trees give place to bushes
Wind-shorn and struggling still
For foothold on the corries
Steep-sloping to the sky,
I want to reach the summit
And watch the clouds race by

The clouds that go so quickly
The whole hill seems to lean
I want to breathe in deeply
The cool air, thin and keen.
My heart turns to high places
All men have long adored —
The proud and lonely mountains,
The Altars of the Lord.

FROM A TOWN WINDOW

From my high-jutting window in town
    Looking down,
The lights constellated burn steady and far;
The purple skies meet with the dark at my feet,
I hardly can tell which is lamp and which star.

And the tall sombre buildings that rise
    Near my eyes
Where one lighted window shines gold in the dark,
Unsubstantial show, that I see them as though
I could walk through the walls without leaving a mark.

And the purring and murmurous choir
    Of the wire
That leads the chained lightning a slave through the street,
In the night-stillness comes like the throbbing of drums,
Like the distant, dread sound of innumerable feet.

THE COLOURS OF LIGHT

This is not easy to understand
For you that come from a distant land
Where all the colours are low in pitch —
Deep purples, emeralds deep and rich,
Where autumn's flaming and summer's green —
Here is a beauty you have not seen.

All is pitched in a higher key,
Lilac, topaz, and ivory,
Palest jade-green and pale clear blue
Like aquamarines that the sun shines through,
Golds and silvers, we have at will —
Silver and gold on each plain and hill,

35

Silver-green of the myall leaves,
Tawny gold of the garnered sheaves,
Silver rivers that silent slide,
Golden sand by the water-side,
Golden wattle, and golden broom,
Silver stars of the rosewood bloom;
Amber sunshine, and smoke-blue shade;
Opal colours that glow and fade;
On the gold of the upland grass
Blue cloud-shadows that swiftly pass;
Wood-smoke blown in an azure mist;
Hills of tenuous amethyst. . . .

Oft the colours are pitched so high
The deepest note is the cobalt sky;
We have to wait till the sunset comes
For shades that feel like the beat of drums
Or like organ notes in their rise and fall —
Purple and orange and cardinal,
Or the peacock-green that turns soft and slow
To peacock-blue as the great stars show. . . .

Sugar-gum boles flushed to peach-blow pink;
Blue-gums, tall at the clearing's brink;
Ivory pillars, their smooth fine slope
Dappled with delicate heliotrope;
Grey of the twisted mulga-roots;
Golden-bronze of the budding shoots;
Tints of the lichens that cling and spread,
Nile-green, primrose, and palest red. . . .

Sheen of the bronze-wing; blue of the crane;
Fawn and pearl of the lyrebird's train;
Cream of the plover; grey of the dove —
These are the hues of the land I love.

BATHING RHYME

Turquoise-green the laughing sea
And the beach is ivory,
Creamy-yellow, creamy-smooth —
How the small waves lisp and soothe!
Those grave woods will not betray,
All the shore is ours today,
There's no soul for many a mile
And the curved waves call and smile,
Coax and whisper and beguile . . .
Quick, your garments cast aside
Go to meet the rising tide!

Childlike run we hand in hand
Down the slope of hard smooth sand,
From the kissing sun's embrace
To the kissing waves that race
Frothing rainbows round our feet —
O the cool shock sharp and sweet!
O the healing of the sea,
Clearer than it seemed to be!
Even clearer — lucent green
Like the eyes of some sea queen.

Looking through the water's shimmer
Can you see a moving glimmer
Whiter than the rippled sand,
White as snow — a beckoning hand?
Dive, and lo! it swings from sight,
Vanishing in broken light.
She is gone, but memories stay
And transfigure all the day;
In the waves' soft touch there lingers
Something of her cool white fingers;

Is that shell her gleaming throat,
That dark weed, her hair afloat? . . .
So her troubling beauty's power
Like the perfume of a flower
Penetrates the sea and air
Making everything more fair:
Pleasure stabbing to the brain
With the joy that touches pain.

Of the water's strength made free,
We're a part of all the sea;
Close its clean caress enfolds,
And each joy that motion holds
Taste we — glad to be alive —
Race the curling waves, or dive
To green dusk, and meet the day
Swift before has passed away
All our crystal pathway thick
With the bubbles rising quick;
Or when that is done we lie
Rocking, gazing at the sky,
Blue and sweet and purely lit
That we gasp to look on it. . . .

Looking through the sunshot deep,
Where our sea-maid lies asleep,
Throat upflung, as white as lime,
With the clear waves keeping time
To the heaving of her breast —
Here we see to veil her rest
Every jewel-tint of green:
Jade, smaragdus, tourmaline,
Beryl and green sapphire's light,
Streaky solid malachite,
Chrysoprase and peacock-sheen
Of the opal's shifting green —
Patched and barred with purple dye

Where the rocks like watch-dogs lie,
Wait crouched beneath the wave,
Hungry, cruel as the grave. . . .

Colour floods our souls until
They must brim and overspill,
Cups too small to bear away
Half the beauty of the day.
But when walking bound with heat
Shackled in the airless street,
When the sky has lost its light
And o'er all the dust is white —
We shall turn to dreams of this
As a damned soul thinks of bliss,
And the loveliness we fail
Now to grasp shall count full tale.

CANTICLE

For the honey-coloured moon, and the shining host of stars,
And the sun's great golden targe,
And the luminous red leaves of the sapling gums in spring,
And the fen-lake's reed-grown marge:

May'st Thou who mad'st all things to be alive,
Thou who hast given the Senses Five,
Thou who hast portioned the Nights and Days,
Thou who hast given us lips for praise,
        Be thanked, Lord God!

For the arrowy swift stream flowing silent in the shade
With its twisting waters green,
For the spray-dewed slender fern-fronds beside the cataract,
The wet black rocks between:

For the pine-tree like a church-spire, that grows upon the ridge,
For the lizard at its foot
That is quicker than a thought, yea, and greener than the moss
Growing round the great tree's root:

For the ocean stretching dark to the clear horizon-line,
For the one white distant sail,
For the ripple and the crisp and the calmness of the bay
With the tide-lines showing pale:

For the bright-eyed life astir in the grave depths of the bush,
For each glimpse of it we get;
For the pattering of rain when the tree-frogs chant in choir
And the glistening leaves are wet:

For the sea of tossing horns when the round-up's at an end,
For the thousand hoofs unshod;
For the blossoms and the bees and the floating butterflies
We thank Thee, O Lord God!

May'st Thou who mad'st all things to be alive,
Thou who hast given the Senses Five,
Thou who hast portioned the Nights and Days,
Thou who hast given us lips for praise,
        Be thanked, Lord God!

SEPTEMBER

The morns are growing misty, the nights are turning cold,
The linden leaves are falling like a shower of gold;
And over where my heart is, beneath the southern sun,
The shearing's nearly over and the spring's begun.

The crying flocks are driven to feed in peace again,
They stream and spread and scatter on the smooth green plain,

40

And in the sky above them the soft spring breezes keep
A flock of clouds as snowy as the new-shorn sheep.

Now later comes the sunshine and sooner comes the dark,
The barefoot newsboys shiver, the ladies in the park
Wear furs about their shoulders, for autumn winds are keen,
And rusty curling edges fleck the chestnuts' green.

The mists hang gauzy curtains of pearl and pigeon-blue
Between us and the distance, the street-lamps shining through
Wear each a golden halo diaphanous and fair —
But not one whit more lovely than my own clear air.

More clear than you can dream it, as bright as diamond
It bathes the plains and ridges and the hills beyond,
It bathes the pillared woodlands that ring with bellbird notes,
With mating calls and answers from a thousand throats.

The lamps are lit in London, beneath their searching light
The smiling anxious faces look strained and very white;
And over where my heart is, twelve thousand miles away,
The dewy grass is glinting at the break of day.

AN OLD SONG

The almond bloom is overpast, the apple blossoms blow.
I never loved but one man, and I never told him so.

My flowers will never come to fruit, but I have kept my pride —
A little, cold, and lonely thing, and I have naught beside.

The spring-wind caught my flowering dreams, they lightly blew away.
I never had but one true love, and he died yesterday.

41

MARCH WINDS

Winds go streaming, shouting loud,
  At their play around the sky,
And my soul is like a cloud
  Blown about with them on high.

Like a hawk unhooded, she
  From my body broke away,
Longing for the company
  Of the winds at holiday.

So she scours the skiey plain,
  Wheeling, dipping in the blue —
Hawk-soul, cloud-soul, turn again!
  What's the lure to use for you?

THE MOON AND THE MORNING

The moon is riding high, the stars are shining
  But very palely, through the clear blue light;
The plain is empty, and the circling mountains
  Rise cold and far through swathes of mist tonight.

There is no wind astir, the serried rushes
  Stand straight as lances round the glassed lagoon;
Within still waters grows a single lily,
  A great white flower of solitude, the moon.

My shadow that seemed taller than the mountains
  Lies gathered at my feet, a pool of ink,
And as I move towards the sombre reed-beds
  I watch it spill and trickle, spread and shrink.

Here in the moon-blanched pasture wide and silent
    With no voice waking and no foot astir
Save mine, the lovely sleeping night surrounds me
    And naught is real save the thought of her.

And yet the plain will wake to green and golden
    Within a few still hours; a breath will pass
Crisping the mirror-surface of the water;
    The larks will start up from the dewy grass;

The proud far sky will smile and grow more kindly;
    The gauzy wisps of cloud that float in it —
The small pale frightened clouds that cast no shadow
    Since they dim not the starshine as they flit —

Will mass to eastward like a host with banners,
    Dawn's dazzling banners streaming out unfurled
Above the dayspring's golden fountain welling
    Up from beneath the dark rim of the world.

SEAGULL

O that these words of mine,
    Leaden and dull,
Shone as your feathers shine,
    Swift-racing gull;

Sped like your arrow-flight,
    Flashing between
All the wide heaven's light
    And the waves' green!

Is it the wind's caress
    Bears you along,

Your white wings motionless,
    Delicate, strong?

No, in a moment more
    Down the steep air
You shoot and whirl and soar,
    Effortless there.

Facing the wind you go,
    Splendid and free,
Dark on the sky you show,
    White on the sea.

Now to the waves you swoop,
    Snatch at your prey —
Smoothly you pause and stoop,
    And are away,

While the sea's rage is spent
    Leaping at you,
Who make high merriment
    Up in the blue.

Then to her calming breast
    That pulses still
You will come down to rest
    At your wild will.

O for the shining word
    Swift as the light,
Showing you, gladdest bird,
    Angel of flight!

SORROW

My Sorrow, O my Sorrow, when first you came to rest
Crouched huddling on my hearthstone, I held you to my breast
And cuddled and caressed you, and rocked you o'er and o'er —
My Sorrow like a baby that creeps upon the floor!

I showed you to my neighbours, I made you rhymes to sing,
For I was proud to own you, the delicate small thing;
And so I nursed you always, till you are grown today,
My Sorrow, like a tiger tense-crouching for his prey.

Yea, silently and swiftly, my Sorrow, you have grown
Till you are waxed so dreadful I dare not be alone —
Alone I dare not face you, lest I be slain outright —
I pray you, monster Sorrow, to sheathe your claws tonight!

DREAMHARBOUR

DUSK IN THE DOMAIN

Elf-light, owl-light,
   Elfin-green sky;
Under the fig trees
   Bats flit by;

Under the fig trees
   Sprawl in a ring
Slim-limbed courtiers,
   Brown Elf King.

Crowned with autumn's
   Tawny gold,
Lizard-eyed, cricket-thighed,
   Neither young nor old:

Like the fig-leaves'
   Broad yellow wreath
Round each forehead — like
   The waves beneath

Lipping the weed-hung
   Low sea-wall —
Ageless, careless
   Lords of all!

Grey rock-monsters
　　Out of the grass
Heaved, lie staring;
　　Moths drift past

On their business —
　　None have the elves,
Who hold high festival
　　By themselves.

　　　　．　．　．　．　．

So I saw them
　　Very plain,
Green-dusky Elfland,
　　Their Domain.

So I saw them
　　As I went through:
Seven slum children from
　　Woolloomooloo!

SUMMER AFTERNOON

Late afternoon streamed yellow still
Into the pleasant kitchen where
Kate, kneeling, polished with a will
The handle of her oven door.
Pretty and pink and thirty-four
Was Kate, and on her bay-brown hair,
Before she rose and stood half shaded,
The sunlight poured its liquid gold.
Her task was done, she was not jaded,
But in her back there came a throb
Of stiffness — well, a kneeling job!
You feel that, when you're getting old. . . .

47

She laughed, the comely youthful Kate,
And laughing, froze; no more alone
She stood and goggled at her mate —
Herself in fifty years, alas
The queer old woman that she was!
Bent, ashen, wrinkled to the bone.

Dry-mouthed, she could not speak, but that
Small wizened woman smiled askew:
'It's nothing, girl, to wonder at;
Even now, we aren't what we have been —
Lord, Lord, the bloom of seventeen! —
And you're not I, though I am you!'

Such a cracked trembling voice! 'Ah well!
We'll meet again, my dear. Good-bye!'

Then a soft empty silence fell,
The clock beneath the dresser shelf
Busily talking to itself
Once more was all Kate's company.

SLEEPING OUT
A STORM AT NIGHT

Wailing comes the south breeze, heralding the gale,
The awning on my balcony is cracking like a sail,
Cracking like a topsail, while beneath the din
My heart is singing to the tune of 'No, I won't go in!'

White-maned horses gallop in the bay beneath,
The trumpet blast has maddened them, the bit's between their teeth:
Now the rain has caught them with a whiplash hiss —
And who would shut himself away from pageantry like this?

Watching drowsy-warm 'twixt ranked veranda bars
The charging massed cloud-cavalry come blotting out the stars,
Streaming manes and pennons swept across the sky —
I ponder, 'Some would rather sleep, perhaps, but never I!'

Just beyond the rain's reach, safe I wait what comes
To shrieking bugle-blasts of wind and thunder's rolling drums,
Purring in my white bed, huddled soft and warm,
While on the whole horizon flares the splendour of the storm.

PITTOSPORUM

Though scarce ten minutes have passed since sunset
    This road has suffered a change;
The moonlight chequers it liquid silver
    And sable velvety-strange;
There is no wind through the soft spring twilight
    But over the garden wall
Deep-scented wave upon wave comes rolling
    To curl and topple and fall:

Fall in my heart and drench it, flood it
    With the sweet of youth, and its ache:
With joy and sorrow half-comprehended —
    They are too much — it will break,
For all the glad things that ever happened
    And all the tragedies too
Are in the scent of the white pittosporum
    Which wakes in the evening dew.

It wakes to more than the dawning's magic,
    To more than the noontide's lure,
Strong with the strength of a tropic forest,
    Voluptuous, virgin-pure.
So all the dreams we forewent

Drift back on us as the sap is rising
    With the slow pittosporum scent:

And echoes wake in the roots of being
    To a sleepy sorcerous tongue
That tells of wonderful things forgotten
    Immortally sweet and young;
It speaks the word of a girl's young dreaming,
    Clear-confident, shy and chaste,
Who sees her life in a glass but darkly
    And will not linger nor haste. . . .

The air is azure, the maid-moon glimmers
    On glossy dark rippled leaves:
Here spring's hope mingles with summer's passion,
    The dumb heart quivers and grieves:
A hundred fragrant small constellations
    Are clustered close on each bough. . . .
Shall ever Age teach me not to suffer
    As needs must I suffer now?

WHITSUNDAY PASSAGE

Wet gold sky and clouds of violet
    Low on the sea's jade-green:
Tumbled islands of sheer chalcedony
    The liner throbs between.

Silver-white are the foam crests dancing
    Over the jade-green sea;
Pale bright gold is the sun-path narrowing
    Out to the West Country;
Colour over me, under, round me —
I lie here like a sea-anemone
    Drawing it into me.

AUSTRALIA

She is a woman tall and brown
  And supple as a swaying vine;
The blood that races in her veins
  Is red and fierce like southern wine.

Her lazy arms are strong as steel,
  She has the gladiator's grace,
The panther's undulating tread
  And tireless velvet-footed pace.

Soft shadows play about her mouth
  Swift curved to smiles, in laughter slow;
Her eyes have that deep tranquil look
  Which far horizons can bestow;

And all things good are hers to give,
  So men will follow anywhere —
Through deserts grim as friendless death —
  The gleaming of her copper hair.

For who has gazed into her eyes
  Is hers while life is in his veins,
She leads him stumbling on beyond
  The dancing heat haze on the plains;

And most she leads to happiness,
  But some to stark defeat, and they
May curse her but they love her still,
  So lasting is her careless sway.

For subtle is her spell and change
  And unawares in sorcery
Enmeshed they stand, while that still witch
  Aloof, smiles half disdainfully,

Since it is not for everyone
   Her lure is cast; not always kind
Her ways, and those rich gifts she has
   Chance-flung, a man must seek to find.

My Lady of the Wilderness,
   With venture in her blood astir!
She bears no gift of peace as yet;
   The lean wild dogs are slaves to her,

And secrets hide behind her eyes
   Of buried rivers no man knows,
Wastes, where one year the lizard starves
   That next year blossom as the rose.

She has no easy calm to give,
   Nor heavy slumber poppy-fed,
The tang of restlessness, the thirst
   Of youth unslaked are hers instead;

And some men do not find her fair,
   But he to whom she once has bent
Her curving, kissing, mocking lips
   Is her sworn soldier, well content

To serve her through the muttering flood
   Through hungry fire and aching drouth,
Because he never can forget
   The wild-fruit savour of her mouth.

She does not lightly show herself,
   But in some traceried forest aisle
Between the writhen branches pale,
   Warm glintings of her sudden smile

Will break on you, or as you lie
   Beside a camp-fire on the plains

Where the throned silence is so huge
   The clanking of the hobble-chains,

The whisper of the flame, the jar
   And crackle as the charred logs fall
But serve to make it stiller yet —
   Then you may hear a dream-dove call,

And, waking, you will see her eyes
   Ashine and sweet and wondering,
Among the stars, and from that night
   You will forgive her anything.

       . . . . .

Let others praise the rose-and-white,
   For rose-and-white is fair to see,
Her smooth brown skin and scarlet mouth
   And tawny hair is life to me.

THE CRAB

A monstrous crab with nippers ready
   Boot-button eyes and goffered back
And stiff mouth set with winnowing feelers
   Like Cancer's in the Zodiac,

After each earthborn man and woman
   Walks sidelong ceaseless night and day.
It creeps and zigzags, darts and scuttles,
   But never halts upon its way.

The golden lads and girls go careless,
   Their elders know with grief or rage,
With backflung glance and thin, forced laughter,
   The monster crab that's called Old Age.

Useless to dodge it or to hurry,
    Useless its presence to deny,
Useless to fight, for it will conquer
    Sure as the sun is in the sky.

Naught but an early death can save us
    From writhing in its grasp uncouth
While that impassive mouth is sucking
    The perfume and the sap of youth,

The lips' red and the gesture's freedom,
    The supple strength of careless limbs,
Eyes, voice — all youth's unheeded treasure
    Under the crab-claw shrinks and dims.

So one by one it marks the rarest
    Sweet subtle morsels to its mind,
Tracking us — here the dry claws rattle
    While grey-wolf Death pads on behind!

And thus before the final struggle
    The bravest man is stripped in part
Of pomps and prides: his surest weapon
    Remains his own unquenched heart.

He can dispute the crab's cold triumph
    And not ignobly find life sweet
Beneath the waving feelers, hungry
    For splendours that it cannot eat.

His is the victory, though he stagger
    Down to the dust where all must lie.
He lives. The crab was never living.
    He has lived, though he age and die.

To us the power and the glory
  Henceforth as since the world began,
The tenderness that's born of courage,
  Of courage in the mind of man.

VISITOR

Suddenly I was broad awake
Staring into the velvety black.
The night was still, still and sweet,
But I knew there was somebody waiting outside
And I had to look, so I padded fleet
Out to the window, thrust it wide,
Pushing the heavy curtain back —
All the sky was a silver lake!

It was the Moon was waiting there.
And all at once she had entered in:
She took possession absolute
And my own little room was no longer my own,
But a royal court where without dispute
She reigned silently, proud and lone,
Snow-quiet feet on the carpet thin,
Blue scarves trailed o'er the broken chair.

IN A FAIR GROUND

Beautiful, good is this garden, where dawn
  Blows through the pine-row like silver trumpets.
  Chorussing birds begin, gay, courageous,
Flirting their wings on the dew-spangled lawn.
Later through clear yellow light come the bees
  Honey-mad, earnest, they throng the hedge whence

Spring breezes carry a scent of daphne
Out to a coppice of delicate trees. . . .
So the sky passes to purple and rose,
    (Black bat-wings cut on its glassy clearness)
    Mopoke and cricket-song, starshine, silence,
Peace over all till the drowsy cock crows. . . .

Save for my questing heart, passionate, blind,
Seeking for that which it never shall find.

SONG IN THE HILLS

Today my heart's a mountain spring
   As clear as diamond, rippling cool,
And if I ask for anything
   Beyond the hour, I'm worse than fool.

Great shining clouds unfold on high
   Like some enormous flower whose stem
Is lost beyond the utmost sky.
   My spirit's leaves unfold with them

Till its last petal is uncurled
   And trustfully it lifts them up,
And all the beauty of the world
   Flows to that small flower's waiting cup.

Why should I ask for anything
   Beyond this swift and simple hour?
Today my heart's a mountain spring,
   My spirit is a wayside flower.

THE OLD GODS

They came into a country new to them,
Our fathers, to a lonely land of light.
'She's virgin,' said they, 'clean and fierce and sweet,
Young as the dawn.' The Oldest Gods were smiling,
Terribly smiling on the bronze-green hills.

Ten thousand thousand shrouded years before
Men builded Babylon and Nineveh
These ruled the new-born and bewildered earth.
Shapes stony-eyed or eyeless, sinister,
Looming through drifts of fog, the cavemen knew
And praised them when the hairy mammoth staggered
Houghed by the stone-axe and the gods' caprice.

And now the saw-toothed peaks are worn to hills
The canons filled to plains, new canons carved
By patient water, and no victims bleed
Upon their altars, but the brooding sense
Of power remains within their ancient kingdom.

We spread its lonely leagues with flocks and herds,
Our ploughs have scarred long miles, but have we tamed,
In these short seven score years, an acre merely?
How quickly these faint scars would fade away
The gods know well. Small wonder that they smile.

By day they bide within the wilderness.
Who is there, entering a silent gully,
That has not, once or often, felt a hand
Constrict his drying throat —? their shadowy priests
Are always watching — or fear's poison drops
Slide chill about his heart, though nothing seen
Threatens or mocks his childish confidence.

So in the daytime. But when twilight comes,
With the first faint star brightening in the west
This land throws off the fetters laid upon her.
Frail bonds and clumsy, and the guardians
Of orchard, garden, field and barn go hence
Back to their gentler motherland, and then
The old grey gods walk clothed in nameless dread
Through this their kingdom, where we nibbling mice
Dream we are lords — this oldest land of all.

The gods are near, but we can never reach them.
They know not love, nor seek it; feed on fear
And blind unwilling worship. They'll not die
While there is food for them, and food shall be
Till the last dog dies on the last man's body.

THE DRYADS OF THE BLUE-GUMS

The bush has many dryad-bands, and all are meet for love,
From the golden-headed little maids who haunt the wattle grove
To those proud sad-hearted dwellers in the sombre sheoaks tall;
But the dryads of the blue-gums are the fairest of them all.

A few are brown as Tongan girls, but most are whiter far,
With a luminous smooth whiteness, than our mortal woman are,
And O the woods are full of them! for only yesterday
I saw alone a little while and watched them at their play.

My trampling through the fern had scared them silent, and they drew
Mouse-still, around their slenderness their filmy scarves of blue —
(But are those soft scarves blue or pink or purple, who can say?
They change beneath our very eyes from violet to grey,
Elusive as that shadow-dance of lavender which falls
In springtime, from the tossing boughs, upon smooth whitened walls.)

But soon those nymphs forgot me quite and thought they were alone
For they were still and very still, but I was still as stone:
So they began to dance again with milky arms upflung
And magic murmured singing in their own sweet unknown tongue.

Now, blinded with their beauty's light, how can I tell it plain,
That swaying, stooping, soaring grace I pray to watch again?
Though close they leaned, their veils half-dropped, and I could see their eyes
Which are as green as beryl-stones, as grey as rainy skies,
I cannot bring the wonder home nor keep it clear and free
A talisman of green and grey — it fades in spite of me.

At night when all the wild things wake, these dryads are not shy
(They have small need of any sleep, their days go softly by) —
Across the pureness of the sky with small pale stars bestrewn,
Above a silver forest, lone there rides the naked moon:
The dryads of the blue-gums all are dancing in her light —
O wistful laughing lovely ones, O wonder-sheen of white,
Clear let me keep the sight of you to guard me as a charm,
A green and silver talisman to hold my heart from harm!

THE MAGIC FOREST

As I went out a-riding one morning in the Spring
When old trees seek to blossom and dumb birds strive to sing,
I found a magic forest of blue-green cypress pine
Night-dark and straight and slender, close set in line on line.

So thick they pressed together across the bridle-track
The branches brushed my forehead, I needs must bend them back,
And therefore duly careful I was no twig to pull,
Remembering that Princess who rode upon a Bull
Through copper woods and silver, and gold woods long ago
And brake one fruit unwitting, and met with bitter woe.

This way and that way swayed I, while pollen of the pine
Upon my head was shaken, red gold-dust, soft and fine;
Yet ever I discovered, with fear but partly feigned,
Some tasselled twig fresh broken that in my hand remained,
And wondered what strange evil would for that theft befall,
Then in a sudden clearing I clean forgot it all.

For gracious there and fragile against the sombre green
The wattle trees were standing, each one a fairy green,
Wrapped in a golden mantle that brighter seemed to shine
Than all the clear Spring sunlight split through the ranks of pine;
Each stood remote and wistful in careless royalty
As though the pines' dark branches were but her canopy.

My heart beat high and quickly for wonder and content,
My horse stepped out more bravely as on again we went;
It is no evil magic that hides among the trees
Of any forest lighted by fragrant flames like these.

SLEEPING OUT

(Eight Years Old)

It's never nice to go to bed,
    But since last year (because
I'm sleeping on the balcony)
    It's nicer than it was,

For half the sky is there to see,
    I lie and watch the stars
Climb up towards the straight black roof
    Past the veranda bars;

The Golden Ship sails by my head,
  (I'd like to get on board)
The Cross stands near, and at my feet
  The Hunter with his sword:

And sometimes when the sea is calm
  The stars shine there as well.
They make long streaky lights, that stretch
  And shiver with the swell.

P'raps, while you're sailing in the stars
  You'll hear a squirling squeal;
And that's a flying-fox, dad says.
  'Gives you a funny feel,

Cold, but not frightened — or a thing
  Sweeps past as quick as light,
Pointed and black — and that's an owl
Gone hunting through the night;

And you've come back on earth to watch
  The branches swish about
Like soft black feathers on the sky,
  Blotting the low stars out.

It's hide-and-seek. And puffs of wind
  Bring spicy scents — oh, far
Far sweeter than the daytime ones.
  I wonder what they are?

One night I woke up awf'ly late,
  And just beside my bed
The moon was rising; very queer
  And upside-down, and red;

Not like our early moon at all —
   Wicked and hot and thin;
The horn that rose out of the sea
   Looked like a red shark-fin.

     .   .   .

I've planned to stay awake all night.
   If there's so much to see
Just in the earliest part of it,
   How grand the rest must be!

I tried to do it all last week,
   But something slips, just when
I'm most awake, and I forget . . .
   And so it's day again.

INTERREGNUM

Little pink clouds like scattered roses
   Over the green translucent sky
Deepen to red as the hot day closes:
   Wavering moths drift by,

Every fragile fairy feather
   Glimmering pale with a borrowed light:
The sun and the moon have fled together.
   What is it shines so bright?

Only the sky, ere the huge night settles
   Drooping black wings, on the earth serene.
See, not a star 'mid the red rose petals
   Shines in that shining green.

MOON-MAID

The lonely moon is drifting high,
A silver bubble in the sky,
   And I should like to go
Following her across the night,
Bathing my body in her light
   That makes it white as snow.

Her sequins glitter on the bay
And well I know how, far away
   Cutting the silk-smooth deep
A big ship's bows move steadily
Making one hollowed wave where I
   Would gladly lie and sleep. . . .

More distant yet, yet in my sight,
The pagan beauty of the night
   Glows where the skies illume
Forests no house-bred man has seen
Where the blue moonfire burns between
   Curtains of velvet gloom.

The night is cool and smooth and bare
As is my skin, my loosened hair
   Is shining like the moon.
Fever and fret and blot of day,
Lo, I have cast them all away —
   What if I find them soon?

Now I shall seek the moon's own land,
A silver girl on silver sand
   I'll dance for her delight;
Forget to love, forget to weep,
Then like a child I'll fall asleep
   Beneath her kisses white.

THE HIGH WOODS

Though we're in a suburb, gay and garden-trim
Everywhere the High Woods, imperially dim,
Lift their crowns above us, rear their shafts on high
From the gully-levels profiled on the sky.

From the laughing fruit-trees' slender laden arms,
From the perfumed gardens' sophisticated charms
We take eager refuge, sure that here at hand
Mounts a sharper fragrance from a wilder land.

Solemn are the High Woods, spite of all the gold
Free-heart sunshine spills there: immeasurably old,
Guarding still the secrets known when trees began,
Therefore how much older than the soul of man?

Though we share no secrets, yet the trees can heal
Surely, and as surely when taut beneath the steel
Groan they in their death-cry, it is echoed low
Thrilling keen within us deeper than we know.

Echoing like a curlew's wail within my breast
I have heard the grieving of a dryad dispossessed,
So I thank the Wood Gods that the High Woods still
Stand untouched, unguarded on the neighbouring hill.

TWILIGHT

At twilight when the crickets chant
    And bats begin to dart and skim
And half the sky is pale and clear
    And all the earth is trembling-dim,
        I love to walk alone — don't you? —
        In case things might be coming true.

I run down to the garden's end:
    The earth smells damp and very sweet:
Nurse doesn't like my going, 'cause
    She says I always wet my feet.
        The crickets stop at once; and when
        I'm past they all begin again.

Between the twisty passion-vine
    And our big jacaranda tree
There is a little curly seat
    Just wide enough to cuddle me.
        I know it by the morning light,
        They never let me stay at night.

It is a very magic place.
    If I could stop there I suppose
I'd see through all those scented leaves
    The story-people coming close.
        I've sometimes felt things just begin —
        But then Nurse *always* calls me in. . . .

THE GREY TERROR

Death creeps about the house at night,
Fumbles our sleeping bodies one by one,
Waits for us in the widening light,
Unseen and watching lingers in the sun;
At each man's elbow all the day
Patient he crouches for his prey,
A great cat pouncing 'twixt soft breath and breath —
Yet I am not afraid of sudden death.

But death-in-life, slow, still and cold,
Mining our treasures; love, hope, faith, all three:
Leaving dry rot where once was living gold

65

And desolation for fertility —
That Death, a gross white-ant queen, spawns
A billion deaths as each day dawns.
She breeds disgust of life and sickly dread.
I fear her, envying the happy dead.

EARTH

Earth puts forth a mingled crop:
   Trees and cities, straight-limbed men —
Shoot and flourish, bloom and drop —
   She receives them all again.

Never greedy, never full,
   She is patient, for she knows
Nothing can escape her pull,
   From the mountain to the rose.

Rocks beneath the air's soft kiss
   Crumble to fertility;
Earth takes back Persepolis
   And the late-born butterfly.

Dust am I that will not rest —
   Pray you, wind, cease not to blow,
Ere she takes me to her breast
   There is much of earth I'd know.

TRUTH

I will not shut my eyes
And lose the light o' the sun
For dread of what Day brings,
Stark terrors, crawling things,
Yea, and the worse that lies
Within me, guessed of none —
I will not shut my eyes.

I will not shut my eyes
But face the ache of light
Whatever shapes show clear
Of loneliness or fear —
Though fire fall from the skies
Until it blind me quite
I will not shut my eyes.

FANCY DRESS

THE WEATHER'S BROKEN

Winter caught a crystal ball:
    Autumn's hand had tossed it
Lightly from her as she went
Hence, for half the year was spent;
Winter nearly let it fall:
    Winter nearly lost it!

Lovelier than any toy
    Winter had expected,
Irised like a pigeon's breast;
Quiet skies and seas at rest,
Every clear and tranquil joy
    Swam on it reflected.

Once a princess had a robe
    Fairy-wrought, together
With her others like the sun
And the shimmering moonbeams — one
Coloured like that crystal globe,
    Coloured like the weather.

Winter held the ball aloft
    Steadily: around them
Golden day and blue still night,

Jasper beads and chrysolite,
One by one went sliding soft
   Down the year that bound them.

Winter stroked her plaything rare,
   Cherished it and kissed it,
Dancing to a measure calm
Tossed it gently, palm to palm;
Tossed it spinning in the air,
   Sprang for it — and missed it.

Crash! the long month's hush is past.
   Thunder, for a token,
Mutters in the stooping sky;
Torn grey veils of rain sweep by,
Trees are writhing in the blast —
   Now the weather's broken.

WINTER IN THE GARDEN

Most of the garden is asleep
   Though leaves are hanging thickly still,
   For night hours bring a frosty chill,
But southern slumber's never deep.

The lovely autumn's hardly gone,
   Yet violets peer warily,
   And roses opening charily
All frosty pink, still linger on.

Green lily buds blanch now to milk;
   The Iceland poppy thrills with sap,
   Shakes off her little furry cap,
Shakes out her skirt of pleated silk.

The snail has sealed his portal well
    With papery white; and folded up
    As smooth as water in a cup
He sleeps within his striped shell.

Down where the little fountain stirs
    Sit doves with feathers all fluffed wide,
    Morose and yet self-satisfied,
Like certain ladies in their furs.

Morning and eve are starry-cool,
    But ever noon is warm with gold.
    Beneath the smoking garden-mould
Brown seeds are swelling to the full.

This garden's sleep is light and brief
    Before the subtle spring's confessed,
    Lightly it takes its hour of rest,
As lightly as unfolds the leaf.

LOOKING FORWARD

What shall I do, my darling, when
Implacable Spring comes by again
With birdsong and boronia's breath
And sure to me as man's sure death
The knowledge that your love is gone —
What shall I stay my heart upon?

Where shall I turn to hide from you?
Little red leaf-buds sticky-new,
And busy blue wrens that trail a stem
Of couchgrass eagerly after them,
Every knot of Spring's silk mesh
Must bind my heart to pain afresh.

70

Eastward through scents and sounds that ache
With sweetness of honey in bush and brake
Blindly I'll turn me, hastening
Towards the sea that knows no spring,
And where the indifferent combers roll
Bathe mind and body and desperate soul.

Salt of our blood and tears is kin
To salt of the sea that watched Life begin:
Her cold voice is less fell than earth's
Harlequin round of deaths and births
And loves containing each: in her
Perhaps I shall find a comforter.

What shall I do when Spring comes by,
Love being dead? I shall not cry
To you, but, till my eyes are clear,
I'll turn my back on the sweet o' the year.
We share no memories of the sea . . .

. . . . . .

You nearly could be proud of me!

LIGHTING-UP TIME

From the western sky quivers
    The last crimson stripe,
And now in Night's orchard
    The fruit's hanging ripe.
Oranges and lemons
    And grapefruit aglow,
What could shine fairer
    Than city-lamps show?

71

STUDY IN GREEN

(Spring morning on Mount Macedon)

There are small bronze catkins on the birch:
Every human soul but I has gone to church,
   But I would have you know that I did not choose to go —
It is not a case of leaving-in-the-lurch.

In a clear still dream I shut my book —
Down the gulley slope to where the hidden brook
   Calls from its mingled screen of the darkest seaweed green
Small green willow-frames are spreading as I look.

Now the larch grows fairer every hour,
A sumptuously sculptured Gothic tower,
   In colour lovelier far than all building stones that are,
A green that strokes the senses like a flower.

Down the long warm shoulder of the hill
Grow primroses and drifts of daffodil
   And forget-me-nots in masses through the jade and amber grasses
Where the lily of the valley's thrusting still.

Pavilions for princesses, and they young,
Are the weeping elms by which a hammock's slung,
   With pistachio-green rosettes broidering their swaying nets
And the periwinkle sky behind them hung.

There's a bold bad robin, and he stands
Where the sycamores are opening little hands:
   He puffs his scarlet chest and he whistles with a zest
That would shame the smartest regimental bands.

Now the air grows sweeter every minute,
All the colour and the breath of springtime's in it;
   O it's glad I am to lie staring upwards to the sky
And having work, and failing to begin it.

Still the bells ring softly from the church:
There are small bronze catkins on the birch:
   Friends, believe me if you may, I'm not idling through the day
But engaged in deep botanical research!

MORETON BAY CHESTNUT

This summer Ann lay dreaming
   For hours and hours and hours
Beneath the chestnut's dome where burned
Apricot and pomegranate
Lemon and persimmon hues;
   Flowering flames or flaming flowers,
Flames to honey-breakers turned
All among the cool green leaves.

This summer Ann lay swinging
Above a floor of flame;
   To and fro her hammock swayed
Above that happy paviment
Coloured like the Spanish flag,
While the honey-eaters came
   Chattering and unafraid
To their lofty banquet-hall.

And through the golden silence
   Their gluttonous sweet song
A myriad bees sang happily,
While the thirsty spine-bills hung
Shrilly calling their delight
   Hour-long, day-long, summer-long,
Darting through the steady tree,
Heels o'er head in the red-gold cups.

This summer Ann lay loving
The pure soft sky that through
   The chinks shone clear as faith, and spilt
Gold drops of sunshine to her gown
Shifting as the hammock swayed.
Leisurely the blossoms fell,
Leisurely the scents that blew
   Between the happy sounds that built
A globe of perfect silence.

IN THE QUEUE

Dusk of a spring Sunday: ferries
   Packed with homing cars,
And a two-mile line of tail-lights,
   Little crimson stars
Like a spotted snake slow-winding
   Through the empty grey
Of the Sabbath streets, and pausing,
   Doubtful, on its way.

         .   .   .   .   .

As we wait there are, thank Heaven,
   Pleasant things to see:
Half the lamps of Sydney sparkling
   Tangled in a tree,
On the harbour's steel-blue mirror
   Far and far below
Jewelled dragonflies and beetles
   Skimming to and fro,
Towering flats, their daylight crudeness
   Mercifully dimmed,
Rising on the blue cloisonne
   Of the skyline limned;
Spires and domes and fairy castles

Climbing up the sky,
While the low last fires of sunset
   Deepen, flare, and die . . .

Now we move — the stars burn brighter
   In the mystic blue —
What will be the next bright dropscene
   Hung before the queue?

A LITTLE DEATH

Only for this I am sorry —
That I should be ill in spring,
When each hour is a separate glory
And the sun's ensaffroning
With its last long rays yields only
Its place to the fairest far
Of the year's young moons — and lonely
For comfort of moon and star
I turn and toss and remember
Past springtimes, and catch my breath —
To be tied to bed in September
Is a faint foretaste of death!

TOWN AND COUNTRY

'Twas when I built my life again
   And came here to the city,
You said 'You'll find it gayer far
   And very near as pretty.
Although the soil is not so red, yet there are gardens here,' you said,
'You will forget how debonair
And tall your country roses were.'

I know I'm very fortunate
    To have a city garden;
My struggling roses do their best,
    But yet — I ask your pardon,
My memory is far too good, I still see how the others stood,
How sweet and full they used to tower,
As if they could not choose but flower.

These flowers, poor dears, are pale and thin,
    And so's the milk men sell us.
Our jersey cow gave milk that would
    Have made their best cream jealous.
I'll not deny it — where's the sense? Town's good, but with a difference.
I shall not bow the knee, not I,
And found my pleasure on a lie.

For there are lovely things enough
    I hardly had expected.
The shiny pavements after rain
    With yellow lights reflected,
The silks in town are brighter far than many sorts of flowers are,
And oh, the distant city light
Abloom upon the purple night!

Yes, when I built my life again,
    I left some pieces lying
That wouldn't fit into the plan
    For all my earnest trying.
I won't pretend I have forgot, nor that they're here — for they are not —
But keep my memories sharp like knives
And thus enjoy two separate lives.

AUSTRALIAN AUTUMN

This is the gentlest season of the year.
   From mists of pearl and gold
   The slow sweet hours unfold
   To crystal colours, still
   As glass, but not so chill.

All birds speak softly in the autumn Bush.
   One bellbird from the deep
   Like a call heard in sleep
   Chimes: in the bronze-gold gloom
   Cool greenhood orchids bloom.

Brown leaves are withering on the alien trees:
   The bronze green of our hills
   Is veiled with blue that fills
   The spirit with a bright
   Sense of intrinsic light.

Now that the dew has vanished, sheep lie down
   By companies content
   In wilga-shade and scent;
   The reaper sounds near by
   Like the cicadas' cry.

And so the mellow day flows on to dusk
   And loveliness that grows
   From skies of mauve and rose,
   While fragrant smoke-plumes lie
   Subtle as memory.

Curled round our hearts in this still jewelled air,
   Risen from the pulsing fire
   Many-hued like desire.
   Overhead, stars blaze white,
   Superb in frosty night.

This is the kindliest season of the year.
   The sun's gold arrows all
   Have lost their barbs: thick fall
   The berries ripe, and still
   The birds may have their fill.

Now peace and plenteousness have spread their wings
   After the blessed rains
   On Autumn's hills and plains;
   We too give thanks and bless
   This southland's graciousness.

PEACEFUL VOICES

I fortunate, I know a refuge
   When the strained spirit tires
Of town's metallic symphony
   Of wheels and horns and wires:

Where through the golden empty stillness
   Cool-flowing voices speak,
The alto of the waterfall,
   The treble of the creek.

From far, beyond the headland's shoulder
   Southeasters bring to me
Reminder of earth's wanderings,
   The strong voice of the sea.

I happy, in a leafy fortress
   Listen to hidden birds
And small waves of a making tide
   Mingling their lovely words.

RAIN MUSIC

As I climbed the mountain, rain was blowing cold,
Grey the sky and mournful, the Silver Falls were gold,
Every bird was silent, yet a chorus rang
Wailing down the gullies, roaring in the trees,
Till it seemed full-throated that the mountain sang —
Cried the organ voices of the wind, and under these
Strains of other music: raindrops lisping chill:
Rivulets that chuckled racing at their will,
Wee frogs fluting treble, big ones chanting bass,
Wheresoever boulders made a sheltered place;
Hoarse sweet hollow voices of the arching fall,
Amber-tawny waters leaping musical.

Other voices too my inner ear heard plain:
Millions in the bushes thankfully held up
Little empty platters welcoming the rain
Millions in the mosses raised a tiny cup
Green or gold or scarlet, to be filled anew,
Brimmed with diamond water, fairer than the dew,
And each one of the millions had a tongue for praise —
O there's music on the mountain these rain-grey days!

WAITING

Faint blue are the distant hills
And the heat haze over the plains
So trembles, they seem to pant
   For the laggard rains.

The trees too swim in a haze
That is bluer than woodsmoke — deep
And slow it curls round their trunks,
   Since the four winds sleep.

79

The earth is wrinkled and old:
None would think that she held at rest
A million million lives
  In her withered breast;

A prison gloomy and bare,
Where a billion grassblades wait
Till the grey rain over the hill
  Shall unlock its gate.

Now great clouds coppery tinged
Throng the far blue field of the sky,
Dazzling bright, but they give no hope,
  For they ride too high.

The cattle hugging the shade
Stand slack, enduring the heat.
Far off, on the plain's straight edge
  Clear, alluring, sweet,

There glimmers a pale mirage —
Such a cool tree-shadowed lagoon
Where we know no water is . . .
  Pray the rain comes soon!

A little cold breeze blows up:
Is it herald of rain, of rain?
We hoped so often before
  And we hope in vain. . . .

Grey clouds from the north and west
Come, cover the staring sky,
Come, rapturous, many-voiced rain,
  Ere the cattle die!

THE TRYST

Autumn was wandering
Far in the South
Slow through patterned vales but now
(Apples burning on the bough)
Berries wreathed about her brow,
Dreams upon her mouth.

Summer, tall lazy lass,
Laughed with us yet
Where down yellow beaches run
Children of the sea and sun —
Thick though trouble's web be spun,
Surfing, we forget.

Slowly towards us walks
Autumn the queen.
Here are scouting clouds that throw
Tender shadows as they go;
Ocean is grape-hued below,
Purple grapes and green.

Humbler small scouts she has,
Netting the ways
Ere the morning gardens stir —
Grim, and wrapped in tabby fur,
Silent spiders herald her
And her dewy days.

Autumn, the gentle one,
Comes north again
To a land too hotly kissed —
(Sharper stars and morning mist)
Autumn keeps her punctual tryst,
Autumn, and the rain!

ON A TASMANIAN ROAD

Though curfew now has sounded for the butterflies and bees,
All the fires of autumn are burning in the trees.
Grey and cold as steel the sky, yet to left and right
Stand walls of polished hawthorn burning bright, burning bright.

Sunset: balsam colours in a brittle crystal sky;
Through the dusk the owls hunt past, hooting as they fly
Small and cold and lonely like forgotten bells;
Streaming down the wind come all the tangled orchard smells:
Woodsmoke, earth and apple-sweet: now the stars burn white —
Hurry home to blazing logs this frosty night!

GREEN DRAGON

One would have thought that you and I
    Were leagues enough apart,
But something turned, when I read your name,
    Heavily in my heart;

A careless phrase, not aimed to hurt —
    Why should it hurt? — a word
That told me nothing I did not know:
    Nevertheless he stirred;

The sleeping dragon in my heart
    Coiled there unknown to me,
Whose green eyes piercing to the deeps of Hell,
    Whose name is Jealousy.

A light word broke his smouldering sleep,
    And he was hard to lull,

He had each fault that a beast could have,
   Save that he was not dull . . .

      .   .   .   .   .

Seeing I've room for things like that
   In my unrestful heart,
Are you not — you are no Saint George —
   Glad that we live apart?

WHITE NIGHTS

A weary thing to do —
To count the long night through
The hours, the hours that tread
With slow unvaried beat,
With heart-heard fateful feet,
Past my unrestful bed.

The nights are long of late . . .
Night after night I wait
And wide-eyed dream of you.
Dreams that no solace lend
Such as the sleep-gods send,
Since even before their end
I know they are not true.

SUFFICIENT TO THE DAY

Herewith I cast away
   The past, the future's load,
Sufficient to the day
   This ribbon of the road
         Unwinding, unwinding

83

Before us as we fly
Past berried hedges burning bright and harvest fields
alive with light
Beneath a clean blue sky.

A cool quick whisper stills
On either side, and dumb
The supple curving hills
Flow past us as we come
Exulting, exulting,
Exulting in our speed
That thus the landscape's coil untwines and melts its
long and gracious lines
To meet the moment's need.

Save for that swift-hushed stir
Of life surprised around
The car's contented purr
Remains the only sound.
In silence, in silence
And clear delight go we,
Such happiness upon us shed, the brown hawks
planning overhead
Are not more proudly free.

The air against our eyes
Streams crystal-cool and bright,
The blue cloud-shadow flies
And we have joined its flight
Forgetting, forgetting
That ever to our shame
Grey dust and weariness have power, with other
things which in this hour
I will not even name . . . .

MISS MERRITT

Miss Merritt was, I have been told,
Not very young nor really old
When, yielding to a mental push,
She thought of building in the bush.
You might deduce from those last words
Miss Merritt nested like the birds:
Not so, alas! She had no wings,
Nor could she make such lovely things
Of woven horsehair, grass, and down
As some birds do. But land in Town
Is dear. . . .
        She found a leafy place
Which she proceeded to deface
In equal measure as she built
And meanwhile had no sense of guilt.
Not from depravity, for she
Was neutral as a soul could be,
Small, grey-eyed, with a palish skin,
Brown hair just fading, pointed chin,
And little hands and feet — but yet
The nightmare's stable that she set
Among the calm and decent trees
Would make your very marrow freeze.

It was a smirking hut, although
She said it was a Bungalow.
It had not that straightforwardness
Which is a hut's most pleasing dress,
But owned upon the other hand
Features no wellbred barn would stand,
A restless roof that did not fit,
With wiggles dangling down from it;
Porch like a frogmouth wide agape,
Weak chimneys of peculiar shape
With aimless bulges low and high

About the walls, the Lord knows why,
Which walls, of course, the builder had
Painted in seven shades — all bad.
Miss Merritt smothered him with praise,
Crowning the labour of his days
With paper roses in a pot,
And called the horror Kozee Kot.

. . . . .

The great trees talked above her head:
'It's bad, but give her time,' they said.
Alas, she added to her sins
By strewing all the bush with tins,
Asparagus and Clingstone Peach
Scattered as far as eye could reach.
She was as cleanly as a cat
In many ways, but not in that.
The trees are kindly people, but
They could not stand Miss Merritt's hut,
So in their low-voiced parliament
It was resolved, with one consent,
That all the land should be Resumed.
And how the lady would have fumed,
If she had known!
         She did not know
Doom brooded on the Bungalow.
Imagination was, in fact,
A quality she wholly lacked.

The trees were kind; they understood
She was not bad, though far from good,
Like almost any one of us
In tram or boat or motor-bus.
They dealt a gentle doom, though strange;
It took three days to make the change,
A pleasing change, yet none the less
It had a kind of awfulness.

The trees drew nearer yet and stooped
Above her hut, her chickens drooped,
Her sleeping pussy twitched his paws:
She said 'It's very close!' because
She felt the thunderous hush of Doom.
She saw enormous branches loom
And blind the stars: she saw them plain
And sighed 'I think we'll have some rain,'
And slept amid the enchanted stir.

Next day her ducks deserted her,
And wild as mallard, journeyed on
To China with the wild black swan.
Her geese, snake-headed, rose to fly
In honking wedges down the sky;
Her cat abandoned his pretence
Of smug domestic indolence
And hunted with the hunting owl;
Her hens all turned to jungle fowl. . . .

Miss Merritt searched each empty shed.
'Perhaps it's native cats?' she said,
But, slightly dazed, she did not care,
And she forgot to plait her hair
That night; so spicy was the breeze,
It called her out among the trees
Barefoot, to listen to a swell
Of chanting fierce and terrible
She felt she ought to understand.

Next day she woke in Fairyland,
Which is, as possibly you know
Superimposed on this one, though
Some people get small joy from thence.
Of Kozee Kot, that rank offence,
Was left no smallest, faintest trace;
Useless for you to seek its place.

But there's a dappled grove, I've heard,
Where, if you sit and speak no word,
You'll see the tufted ears of that
Which was Miss Merritt's portly cat,
A lean bewhiskered scoundrel now;
And from the highest cedar's bough
Stout Orpingtons, grown lithe and wise,
Salute the dawn with lilting cries.
And watch the greatest tree of all —
They say it may with luck befall
That you shall see Miss Merritt flit
A gold-bronze Dryad, out of it
In ageless beauty bare and free. . . .

. . . . .

She never has appeared to me.

THE WAITING LIFE

Since it befell, with work and strife
I had not time to live my life
I turned away from it until
Work should be done and strife be still.

My hands and head for use are free,
Nor does my own life worry me,
But docile as a spaniel waits
Until this present stress abates.

Tranquil it breathes, and waits, I know,
With all its joy contained. But oh
I hope when I have time to play
My life will not have run away!

GORSE BLOOM

When the gorse is out of bloom
Kissing's out of season.

Old Rhyme.

O what has happened in my heart this grey and windy day?
The thousand little voices there, what do they sing and say?
They make a joyful clamour like the dawn-awakened birds,
A brave triumphant chorus, but I cannot tell the words.

This lonely road runs barrenly beside the leaden sea,
And is it that I'm born again, or what has come to me?
It seems a spell has lifted now that bade my blood run slow
This long time, for it's flame today — but who could hate me so?

The grey clouds stood above my head, but all the world is fire,
And O, if only you were here, my love and my desire!
For see, beside the highway that was barren as the tomb
Even the harsh and dusty gorse is breaking into bloom:

At last, at last the tide has turned, at last the spell is broken,
And thousand thousand tongues of flame are lighted for a token
That kissing is in season and true love may take its course,
Whether that course be smooth or rough — the bloom is on the gorse !

A MATERIALIST

When darkness brooded on the deep
    And all the earth was bond to fear
Of things unknown and powerful,
    His sires saw Terror all too near,
The dread that gripped their quaking souls

Has reached him in another form,
　Warning, as distant bells toll clear
　　In the dark hush before a storm.

Because his great-great-grandsire's soul
　　Sickened at corpse lights in the fens,
And hedged itself with spells and charms
　　More tremblingly than other men's,
He holds, says he, to solid things,
　　And categorically denies
The truth of what he cannot see,
　　Finding it good to shut his eyes.

Never a legend was so wild
　　But that it held some errant touch
Of life, but this man doubts of all
　　Because his kind believed too much.
Never a medicine-man so false
　　But that amid his pattering
Once in a while his lying lips
　　Were brushed by Truth's impartial wing;

But this man, lest the faithful earth
　　Should once again beneath his feet
Fail as it did in ages past
　　Shuns certain hidden things and sweet,
Denying all beyond man's grasp,
　　Though in man's blood, 'For,' reasons he,
'If neither God nor Devil were,
　　How very safe a man might be!'

His hag-rid ancestors that heard
　　Warlocks and witches on the blast
Have cheated him of many joys,
　　Their voices warn him from the past,
And with protective common sense
　　He turns from paths that smile to us,

And will not play with thoughts of fauns,
    Remembering them dangerous.

So, fettered by the fear of fear,
    His fancy runs not free like ours.
Lest there be demons in the rocks
    He sets no fairies in the flowers.
There's much in him to interest,
    But that which takes my humour most
Is the defiant voice of dread
    In which he'll speak about a ghost.

THE MOVING MOUNTAIN

Our train was moving slowly when but two short miles away
I saw the mountain crouching like a shaggy beast of prey.
Our train began to hurry home, as summer night was falling.
The mountain moved beside it like a stealthy monster crawling.
He easily kept pace with it and never had to hustle,
I could have sworn beneath his fell I saw the rippling muscle.
The panting train took fright at last, upon its tracks it doubled,
And lo, the mountain lay inert, his huge repose untroubled.
I'm glad he didn't pounce on us, there isn't any doubt
That if he had, the Northern Mail would have been flattened out —
With one blow of his mighty paw, the while it whistled shriller
That mountain would have squashed it as a cat a caterpillar!

IMPRESSION — SPRING WEATHER

Here's the land of milk and honey 'was promised us of old —
Tall silver blue-gums ankle-deep in wattle gold;
Grey clouds and thunder-blue and shaken white,
A hillside trembling in the thin spring light,
Light that's blowing from a stormy sky like silver-shot silk —
The wattles like honey and the gums like milk.

ONCE WHEN SHE THOUGHT ALOUD

I've had all of the apple, she said,
    Except the core.
All that many a woman desires —
    All and more.
Children, husband, and comfort enough
    And a little over.
Hungry Alice and bitter Anne
    Say I'm in clover.

I've had all of the apple, she said.
    — All that's good.
Whiles I feel I'd throw it away,
    The wholesome food,
Crisp sweet flesh snowy-cool, and skin
    Painted bright —
To have a man that I couldn't bear
    Out of my sight.

PICNIC DAY

For weeks we thirsted for its coming —
   Childhood's long weeks that stretch like years —
Until at last it dawned in glory,
   The crowded day of hopes and fears.

Full half the sky was curtained crimson;
   Sleepy, Nurse helped us dress; athrill
We walked through unfamiliar shadows
   Beachwards; the sun's rim topped the hill.

Old Sam was waiting at the jetty,
   Gnarled as a vine-stock, cherry-lipped.
'Fine day mum! 'mornin', mate, no hurry!
   Go easy till the tucker's shipped!'

Wriggling, we watched those lagging grown-ups
   Slow, slow as treacle, stow away
Our picnic baskets in the dinghy —
   We wanted to begin the Day.

Small gilded waves came dancing towards us
   And slapped the keel, turned beryl-clear,
And made a lovely sunshot shadow;
   The rowlocks creaked; our Day came near!

Across a sparkling stretch of harbour,
   Diamond-pure in morning light,
Grave as a child himself, Sam rowed us;
   Until our white beach came in sight

Round Bradley's Head, we other children
   Joy-rapt, stirred neither foot nor hand,
But we leapt yelling from the dinghy
   Before her nose had ploughed the sand.

And up the beach, the dry sand squinching
   Beneath our feet, to choose a place
To cast our shoes and stockings from us,
   We ran a headlong, desperate race.

We ran to meet the dancing water,
   And through it watched our white feet, clad
In shifting golden scales of sunlight
   As bright as ever mermaid had.

Each rosy wilderness of rockpool
   We pored upon, its life to see,
Then on the velvet surface ironstone
   Our bare feet clung voluptuously.

Pink shells and purple, crabs and starfish,
   And lovely nameless mysteries
We gathered, dropping them to tickle
   The fruitlike sea-anemones.

The royal day went by like music,
   We never paused to hear it pass,
Not even as we ate ambrosia,
   Sprawled idle on the wiry grass.

Then home at dusk, our fingers trailing
   In dark waves tipped with phosphorus fire,
Each sleepy salty head still humming
   With tunes of satisfied desire.

Ah, it was over, over, over,
   The longed-for day of our delight,
But, soaked with scents and sounds and colours,
   We all possessed the sea that night.

Before our closed eyes flamed the beaches
   And jewelled rockpools all night long,
And through our dreams the waves came chanting
   Their everlasting marching song.

SKETCH-PORTRAIT OF A LADY

    Supple and slim
As a fountain-plume jetting
Skywards and murmuring the lilies among;
    With a rhythm of limb
That goes balancing, swaying,
Flowering to beauty immortally young.

    Green dusky eyes
Like the sky after sunset,
West, where its beryl is lit with a star,
    Mocking and wise
Their inscrutable clearness,
Fringed with the dark, seeing keenly and far.

    Sombrely gold
Like bush-honey slow-dripping,
Pungently sweet flows her voice through each word;
    As her free thoughts unfold,
They are worthy, no question,
To fledge in her feathers, my Paradise-bird!

    O, but the best
Of her glories and graces
She the elusive not lightly will show.
    Hid in her breast
In the tenderest, warmest,
Proud loyal heart that a friend needs to know.

THE WINGS OF A DOVE

I must rest a little while:
Whither shall I go?
Which shall be my sanctuary
Of hundreds that I know?

There is a mountain gully brimmed with trees
    So old, so grandly tall, that there
The giant tree-ferns clustering at their feet
    Seem frail as maidenhair;
The sea-green moss is velvet underfoot,
    I look through sea-green air
Upwards to lace of leaves, and onwards still
    To see a sheer stream drop
    In silver curtains from the mountain-top.
I'll stay and watch the flying rainbows swoop
    About that waterfall
With a friend who answers thought —
    Or nobody at all.

There is a cliff that faces towards the East.
    Kingfisher-blue, kingfisher-green,
Clear water swings beneath it muttering
    The brown bright rocks between.
Landward the harsh wind-carven bushes make
    Against the world a screen,
A screen from half its winds and all its web;
    And through the bright air croons
    The sea its secret everlasting runes.
I'll listen to the breathing of the waves,
    The querulous seagulls' call,
With a cheerful Cocker pup —
    Or nobody at all.

There is a hanging wood that covers half
    A Wiltshire hillside that I know,

A leafless wood, dim purple, looming on
    The landscape dumb with snow.
We are the last survivors of mankind;
    Around us as we go
There is no sign of life; no sound except
    The crinching crisp and sweet
    Of virgin snow beneath our careless feet;
I'll stay here till the darkening sky has dropped
    Its muffling velvet pall
With a green-eyed woodlander —
    Or nobody at all.

I know a long lagoon on Northern plains
    Where small white everlastings shine,
Where lovely things are happening all day long
    And that hour shall be mine
When level sun rays on a day of spring
    The throngs incarnadine
That come to drink: ibis and pelican,
    Parrots in patchwork dresses,
    Egrets like slender sad bewitched princesses;
I'll watch the hunting swallows and the teal
    And pearl-grey brolgas tall
With a brother or a horse —
    Or nobody at all.

High noontide in the Valley of the Kings:
    A hawk sails proudly overhead,
The one fleck in this tawny solitude,
    For all the ancient dead
That men have left here, keep a narrow state
    Each on his sculptured bed
Where never sun can reach them, or the glow
    Of this Egyptian blue:
    A flame to warm the granite coffins through —
I'll gaze at peace from this scant lilac shade
    Beneath the stark rock-wall,

One lean knight for company,
  Or — nobody at all.

I am lucky who can fly
To kingdoms of my own
With a picked and perfect friend
Or preferably, alone.

THE JUNGLE

We bring strange blossoms from our dreams
  And wilder yet we leave behind,
So strange we dare not look on them
  With the cool daylight mind.

Red monstrous orchids hairy-lipped
  Swing low from boughs we cannot see,
So high they are, and unknown birds
  Flutter from tree to tree.

Crying with their soft human tongues
  Some message that would make us wise,
Could we but understand, while all
  The brake is quick with eyes.

Flowers press high about our knees,
  But melt within the hands that clutch.
The weed that grows on Lethe's wharf
  Is not more vague to touch:

Or, rooted in ancestral slime,
  One magic lily blue and proud,
That at the earliest breath of dawn
  Fades changing, like a cloud.

The twilit jungle of our dreams
　　Is rich unthinkably, for what
Is all the life we know in it
　　To that we have forgot?

CLIMBER'S JOY

A pathway climbs on the mountain's flank,
　　It elbows up like a Z.
At almost any kink of the way
　　You can see two turns ahead.
Here are steps in the living rock,
　　Here is a bloodwood bridge,
And here is an alley of sand that leads
　　To the pink-white quartz of the ridge.

But there wasn't a path where *I* came down,
　　There wasn't a sign to guide.
The woven bracken clutched at my hand
　　The grass-trees whispered beside.
Sliding down from a slippery ledge
　　Into a myrtle-tree —
The tougher the varied barriers are
　　The greater pleasure to me.

Not that I think I climb so well,
　　Not that I do not know
How light the mountain has let me down —
　　But that it's good to go
Using all of my flowing strength,
　　Every muscle and nerve,
Speed and balance and judging eye
　　All eagerly fit to serve . . .

FORERUNNER

Chrysanthemums in an orange jar,
　Russet and golden, sharp of scent,
Breathe of frost-nip and burning leaves,
　Berry-harvest and birds' content:
Thick white dews of the autumn morning,
　Mist-wreaths airily vanishing —
And one narcissus-wand born untimely
　Smells of spring.

One frail stem with those carven leaves,
　Five pallid stars against the blaze
Bronze and gold, of the autumn flowers —
　Riches piled for the cooling days;
Five pale stars, but their troubling perfume
　Takes the heart with its ageless fret.
Autumn is strong, but the thrust of springtime
　Stronger yet.

FLOWER OF THE GORSE

Winter is a sober time,
　Shand's a sober village:
Leafless trees and faded grass,
Sombre leaf-brown tillage —
Beetle faces moon and pass,
　But, with the Spring
Golden glory spills itself
　Over everything.

Over every hedgerow
　Little flamelets dart,
Shining like the kingly sun,
　Comforting the heart;

All the earth is quick with gorse,
    Bounteous the yield,
Golden billows toppling
    Into every field.

From a grove of coconut
    From an isle of spice
Heady scents blow over Shand,
    Change it in a trice;
Never lass so homely but
    Magic haloes her,
Never lad so dull but now
    Feels his heart astir.

Are they mad when Spring comes by?
    They have golden reason.
When the gorse is out of bloom,
    Kissing's out of season.
Never day without its flower
    Through the changing year —
Now behold the unbroken gold!
    Kissing season's here!

          .   .   .   .   .   .

One there was who loathed the gorse,
    Would have beaten down
Every little tongue of flame
    All about the town;
Lank Master Snuff-the-Sin,
    Censor self-appointed
Of the village ways and words —
    He the Lord's anointed!

So last year he preached and stormed:
    'Keep the village clean!
Rid the field and road of gorse,
    And the ditch between!'

All the people were abashed,
    Yielded to his will,
Hacked and dug and burned it out —
    Kissing's hard to kill.

'Hack them out and burn them down,
    Purify the place!
Ill weeds, ill weeds,
    Growing up apace!'
Scowling at the sweethearts,
    Gloating on his duty,
Hating not the greedy gorse
    But its wasteful beauty.

Piles of prickly brush there are
    Brown and dry and dead,
But in every field the gorse
    Rears a vivid head.
Dauntless is the gorse-bush,
    Every little slip
Points a sturdy finger
    Burning at the tip.

Is the sunshine killed by cloud
    Where the thunder rides?
No, but black amid the gorse
    Sullen Hatred strides,
Slashing with his crookstick,
    Hacking at the roots,
While unconquered gorse yet
    Puts out flowering shoots.

Happy lovers dumb as stars
    Heed him not at all,
Gorse swings censers in the breeze

As for festival:
Sour hearted Slaughter-Joy
    Will be soon forgot,
Life, impartial,
    Thrives and slackens not.

SANDRA'S PROTEST

I am not wasteful, Goodman Gill,
    Not wasteful, no.
I use and give and spend and spill
    Along the way I go.

I waste no chance of joy at least,
    Nor thrust away
Untasted at Life's changing feast
    One salted hour of day.

Though well I knew that ships might wreck
    (And mine went down)
I twisted pearls about my neck
    And wore a gleaming gown

To please my lover as we supped,
    Nor locked them fast
Where moth and envious rust corrupt
    And thieves break through at last.

          .   .   .   .   .

Sure it is waste to put Joy by
    Unused, unshared,
Lest Death come laughing noiselessly
    And take you unprepared;

Lest Death come with his silent stride
    And Joy is gone
With you and carefulness beside —
    A jest to think upon!

FANCY DRESS

'Last night the moon had a golden ring —'

She smiled behind a lawny cloud,
    A Tudor lady in a ruff,
A chubby Holbein, douce and proud.
    Starchy, but genial enough.
Wide ring on ring of lawn and lace
Spread round her inexpressive face,
Which yet was deeply memorable —
Lady, the Holbein type wears well!

SPRING SONG OF SYDNEY

Spring has come back to this Sydney of ours;
All the deep gardens brim over with flowers;
All the steep gardens climb down to the harbour
Frothing with blossom on trellis and arbour.
Clematis, jasmine, wistaria, rose,
Who can keep tale of the pageant that goes
Scented and hued like the suite of a bride
Towards the delphinium-blue of the tide?

Hark to the magpie there! and in the hush
Now the sun's riding high — listen, a thrush!
Soon, soon the locust will silence their song,
Spring is swift-footed but Summer broods long.

THE WEAK POINT

Say not 'She loves too much,' of her
　　Whose love is a consuming flame
Destroying god and worshipper.
　　　Not love but lack of wit's to blame.
　　　　For, if we put it to the touch,
　　　　No one has ever loved too much.

Say not 'He was too strong,' whose rough
　　Cold power men's fortunes overthrew;
A giant's strength were scarce enough
　　For all that mortals have to do.
　　　　Great gifts he had: it was his small
　　　　Honour and mercy ruined all.

Then why should man distrust the deep
　　Hid flint and steel within his soul
And fire that from the two may leap?
　　More love, more strength we need; the whole
　　　　Of life's there: greater perils lie
　　　　In lack than superfluity.

PRUDENCE

She thought that trouble was coming,
　　So hid away
And locked the door of her heart against
　　The light of day.

At dusk she ventured — 'What happened?'
　　A neighbour mocked:
'Joy paused by you at the height of noon —
　　Your door was locked.'

ANOTHER HERITAGE

Not long ago,
Only three lives ago,
Half of my blood ran warm in northern weather
On a far strand
In a grim lovely land
Shrouded with mist and glorious with heather.

Though this gold sun,
This careless spendthrift sun,
Soaks through my body drenching it with light,
Yet to the North
From whence my sires went forth
Swift thoughts go thronging to a winter's night

Bitter and dark,
When the relentless stark
Trumpeting stormwind eddied ceaselessly
Like a cold stream
Sundering dream and dream
Round some grey house beside the western sea.

Mist on the blue
Hill, speaks of what I knew
Once better far than these wide sunny lands.
Deep in the brain
Something turns back again
To the accustomed thing it understands.

Dark memories
Run north beyond the seas
To Kentish orchard snow, green Irish hill,
But the north land
Gives cragsman's foot, and hand
Unpractised, groping for forgotten skill.

That skill long since —
How many ages since!
Hands gone to dust have gathered, stored and spent,
Blindly today
Gropes on its subtle way,
Striving towards new use and full content.

Came the great wind,
The wandering venturer wind,
One year, to blow the northern seed apart
Rooting it here
In a great land and dear,
Not to forget you, Highlands of my heart.

Not long ago,
Only three lives ago —
It is too little for a soul's forgetting.
Mountain and sea
Are magic food to me
Since I have known them in another setting.

PICTORIAL ACKNOWLEDGEMENTS

The publishers wish to express their gratitude to the National Gallery of Victoria, and the Art Gallery of New South Wales for permission to reproduce the paintings in this collection.

PLATE 1 (opposite page 28)
Charles Conder (1868-1909)
The Farm, Richmond 1888
Oil on canvas 44.4 x 50.9
National Gallery of Victoria
Purchased with assistance of
a special grant from the
Government of Victoria
1979-1980

PLATE 2 (opposite page 29)
David Davies (1862-1939)
Evening Templestowe 1897
Oil on canvas 44.9 x 55.8
National Gallery of Victoria
Purchased with assistance of
a special grant from the
Government of Victoria
1979-1980

PLATE 3 (opposite page 36)
Julian Ashton (1851-1942)
A Corner of the Paddock 1888
Watercolour on board 40.5 x 58.8
National Gallery of Victoria
Purchased with assistance of
a special grant from the
Government of Victoria
1979-1980

PLATE 4 (opposite page 37)
Charles Conder (1868-1909)
Coogee 1888
Oil on board 26.8 x 40.6
National Gallery of Victoria
Purchased with assistance of
a special grant from the
Government of Victoria
1979-1980

PLATE 5 (opposite page 76)
Rupert Bunny (1864-1947)
A Sunny Noon c. 1913
Oil on canvas 65 x 40.3
National Gallery of Victoria
Purchased with assistance of
a special grant from the
Government of Victoria
1979-1980

PLATE 6 (opposite page 77)
Frederick McCubbin (1855-1917)
Cottage, Macedon c. 1895-1897
Oil on canvas 46.4 x 25.4
Art Gallery of New South Wales
Purchased 1962

PLATE 7 (opposite page 92)
Sir Arthur Streeton (1867-1943)
Near Heidelberg 1890
Oil on canvas 52.1 x 39.5
National Gallery of Victoria
Felton Bequest 1943
Reproduced by courtesy
of Mrs M. H. Streeton

PLATE 8 (opposite page 93)
Tom Roberts (1856-1931)
Mentone 1887
Oil on canvas 50.2 x 75
National Gallery of Victoria
Purchased with the assistance of
a special grant from the
Government of Victoria
1979-1980